Pit Road Pets: The Second Lap
NASCAR Stars and Their Pets

Photography by Karen Will Rogers
Stories by Wendy Belk

A Ryan Newman Foundation Publication

Publisher: Ryan Newman Foundation (Ryan and Krissie Newman)
Project Manager: Krissie Newman
Photographer: Karen Will Rogers
Retoucher: Vincent A. Brown
Writer: Wendy Belk
Editors: Annette Vanderhoff and Kathy Halik
Assistant Editor: Mary Svanson
Design and Print Production: Dina Dembicki Graphic Design
Cover Design: Russ Wright

Ryan Newman Foundation
P.O. Box 5998
Statesville, NC 28687
www.ryannewmanfoundation.org

Pit Road Pets
www.pitroadpets.com
info@pitroadpets.com

The Ryan Newman Foundation will be donating a portion of its proceeds from
this book to the Humane Alliance in Asheville, North Carolina to supplement the
income for those who can not afford to have their pets spayed and neutered. The
Humane Alliance will work with the ASPCA to give grants to their spay/neuter clinics
throughout the nation. These clinics will provide much needed support in their
communities and help fight pet overpopulation. The other proceeds will help the Ryan
Newman Foundation to build an animal and education center in North Carolina.

The Ryan Newman Foundation is a 501 (c) (3) nonprofit organization.

This book is dedicated to the abandoned and homeless pets at animal shelters across the world.

Contents

Contents

Foreword

by Mike Arms

It is a special treat for me to be asked to write this introduction for *The Second Lap* because it is near and dear to my heart to reflect on the special bond between humans and animals. I have spent more than 30 years working to protect the lives and ensure the welfare of orphaned animals and I know first-hand of their incredible capacity for love and how they enrich our lives.

My journey started back at an animal facility on the streets of New York where an event took place that would change my life forever. It was only days before I was to leave my position to escape the cruelty inflicted on animals and the daily heartbreak that I had to witness, when I received a call that a dog had been hit by a car and there was no driver available to pick him up. I quickly took off my suit jacket and put on a driver's jacket prepared to rescue an injured dog that would require immediate medical attention. As I arrived to the scene I saw a small black and tan dog that had been hit hard by a car and whose back was literally broken. He lay in pain unable to move, so I ran to his side and cradled him in my arms.

At that moment, I heard someone calling to me from the doorway of an apartment building. I turned and three men standing there demanded to know what I was doing with the dog. I told them that I was taking him to safety and wanted to know if it was their dog. They said it was not but they were betting on how long it would live. Horrified, I turned and began to put the dog into the ambulance, but at that moment the men attacked me with a bat and a bottle. They beat me and stabbed me until I

lay unconscious in the street. Although it seemed impossible, the little black and tan dog crawled to my side and licked me awake. As I lay in the street with my little friend, I begged God for another chance in life. If granted, I would dedicate my life to animals. Moments later he crossed over Rainbow Bridge and some day we will meet on the other side and take that walk that was meant to be. To this day I have kept my promise.

I know that my little furry friend laid the foundation for the rest of my life. The bravery and compassion that he showed to me that day helped me to see that I had a purpose in life and that purpose was to save as many orphaned animals as I could before my time was up. Animals give so much of themselves to us each and every day and we do so little in return to protect them and ensure their well-being and safety. When I think of the rescue dogs of 9/11, seeing eye dogs, police dogs, service dogs, and so many others that simply provide protection, comfort, and company to those who are limited in their capabilities, I can't help but feel that we can do more and we need to do more to improve their quality of life.

Today, I am working to change the future of animal welfare with my home base at Helen Woodward Animal Center in San Diego. Whether creating innovative adoption programs to place over 3,000 animals a year or training other organizations to stop the euthanasia and start actively marketing their animals to increase adoptions, I am committed to stopping the killing and giving these beautiful animals a chance to live.

The Iams Home 4 the Holidays program which was created at Helen Woodward Animal Center in conjunction with the Iams Company 10 years ago has now placed over 3 million orphans and is poised to find homes for another 1.5 million for the 2009-2010 holiday season. These loving orphans deserve a home and second chance at happiness and it is my goal in life to ensure they get it.

I love *The Second Lap* so much because it really focuses on the love between the NASCAR community and their pets and the way that they enhance each other's lives. Clearly they are much more than just companions – they are truly family members and that really touches my heart. A beloved best friend like these pets can truly carry you through the best and worst of times with their steadfast devotion and unconditional love.

As you enjoy this book, remember all of the orphans who are not lucky enough to be someone's best friend and who are still waiting for their forever home here at Helen Woodward Animal Center and other facilities across the country. Your purchase of *The Second Lap* will help provide for the vital resources that keep adoption programs running, from veterinary supplies to vaccinations. In a small way you can tell the orphans that they are not forgotten and that someone cares about them even if the rest of the world has turned their back on them.

Thank you for your love of animals and for caring enough to make this purchase today. I hope you take this opportunity to not only celebrate the special bond between people and pets, but also appreciate all that our animal friends do to enhance our quality of life. 🐾

Introduction

by Krissie Newman

My husband, NASCAR driver Ryan Newman and myself formed the Ryan Newman Foundation in 2005. We became aware of an epidemic across our nation where millions of animals were abandoned, homeless, and euthanized in our shelters. People were reaching out for help, not only for themselves, but for all the animals that were being mistreated and uncared for. Ryan and I decided to try to make an impact, educate people about animal welfare, and encourage people to have their pets spayed or neutered. It was our relationship with those in the NASCAR community that made this effort possible. In 2006, we published our first book; *Pit Road Pets: NASCAR Stars and Their Pets*. With the first print run of 20,000 copies selling out, we obtained sponsorship and were able to re-print another 20,000. Amazing for first time publishers who were originally told that NASCAR fans do not read! Thank you for helping us prove them wrong.

It is because of the fans, that we decided to do this second edition. Not only will you find stories from other NASCAR drivers, crew chiefs, team owners, media personalities, and event directors, you will find pictures and faces of what makes our sport so great, the fans. Our team traveled to a few NASCAR racetracks, and we were amazed to find how many fans of our sport had their pets traveling with them. We hope you enjoy the stories and photos you will find in this book, as much as we have enjoyed creating it. To many of us, our animals are not just pets, they are our family.

The proceeds from the first book helped build a regional spay/neuter clinic at the Humane Society of Catawba County in Hickory, NC. The Ryan Newman Foundation S.N.I.P. clinic has already performed over 13,000 spay/neuter surgeries since their doors opened in 2007, preventing the death of hundreds of thousands of unwanted and stray animals.

The Second Lap is going to make an even bigger impact on these numbers. The proceeds will be going to projects within animal welfare. Creating grants for the Humane Alliances spay/neuter clinics throughout the nation. These grants will provide funding for those who cannot afford the low cost spay/neuter services, yet still want to keep their pets healthy and safe. The rest of the proceeds will be used to create an animal center in North Carolina that will serve as a model for animal welfare and education throughout the U.S.

If you would like to read more about the Ryan Newman Foundation, and our other foundation projects, we invite you to visit our web site at www.ryannewmanfoundation.org.

Thank you for supporting the Ryan Newman Foundation by purchasing *Pit Road Pets: NASCAR Stars and Their Pets*, and *Pit Road Pets: The Second Lap*. 🐾

Justin Allgaier
Mercedes and Daisy Duke

"**B**oth Ashley and I had pets when we were kids. I had a fish, which some people don't count as a real pet. I also had a rabbit named Buttons.

"Ashley had cats and dogs when she was a kid. Ashley's mom was an x-ray assistant at a veterinarian's office where we lived, so I think her love for animals was just natural.

"When we decided that we wanted a pet, we both had our own ideas on what we wanted. Ashley wanted small dogs that would be good to keep inside the house, and I wanted dogs that would travel well with us, especially since we were going to races all over the country. We decided that Chihuahuas fit both of our criteria.

"Since we did travel so much, we thought it would be good to get sisters so they could keep each other company. That's how we ended up with Mercedes and Daisy Duke, who are three-years-old and spayed.

"One of the cool things about Ashley's mom working at a vet's office, she has all the answers if we ever have a question about the dogs.

"Mercedes is all black with short hair. I had always wanted a black Mercedes, so when we got the all black dog, it just seemed fitting to name her Mercedes. Mercedes keeps us entertained because when she feels like it, she can run just like a Greyhound. It is hilarious.

"Daisy Duke is a black and brown Chihuahua with much coarser hair than her sister. Daisy Duke is kind of like the "mother hen" of the two dogs. When Daisy Duke doesn't see Mercedes, she gets very concerned. Daisy Duke will wander all over just aimlessly looking for her sister until she finds her. Daisy Duke's favorite thing is to rollover on her back so we can rub her belly.

"The dogs have been great companions for us, and it's pretty fitting that, since racing is such a big part of our lives, their birthdays are during Speedweeks while we are in Daytona." 🐾

Justin with wife Ashley, and dogs Mercedes and Daisy Duke

 Pit Road Pets **1**

AJ Allmendinger
Misty Marley

"**I** grew up with dogs. My first dog was Britney – a Pit Bull. She would go to the racetracks and go-kart races with me. When she was there, I wouldn't have to set an alarm because I would wake up at 5 in the morning with her staring over the top of me. I'd open my eyes, kind of point for her to go and would say "go get mom and dad." She would run and jump into the other room and get them up.

"At the go-kart races everybody knew Britney. Unfortunately, she had bad hips and had to have a couple of surgeries on them, so she would be in her cast walking around at the racetrack. It was really sad, but she didn't let it stop her. She was so popular that every time she had a cast on, all the drivers would sign her cast.

"A couple of years ago, Lynne and I decided we were going to get our own dog. We were looking for a dog because my wife says I am way too immature to have kids. Misty was perfect because she had a lot of energy and I needed a dog like that because I have way too much energy.

"Misty Marley is what we call her because she was in the movie 'Marley and Me.' We know for sure that one part of the movie she was in was when she steals Jennifer Aniston's underwear and runs through the screen door because she actually does that with Lynne all the time now.

"The other one was when the food spills all over the ground, and she is sprawled across the floor eating it. That's Misty too, for sure.

"Misty is just a great dog in general. There's a little park by our house with slides and swings, and when we first got Misty we started walking her over there. When she was a puppy, I put her in a little swing. It was cute. That's why she's Daddy's Little Girl.

"She slides down the slides – except for the big twisty slide. It's pretty funny. She does not like that slide. I think as a puppy, we slid her down and she didn't like that one so much. But the slides that go down straight, she loves.

"Her other favorite thing is chicken. Honestly, Misty is fed better than any person in the world. My favorite food is chicken. I'm always eating chicken. So anytime, whether it is dinner at a restaurant or Lynne is making it, Misty is sure to get her own dinner. Any day I eat chicken, Misty is eating chicken. I wish I was spoiled like that.

"Before we got Misty, Lynne and I had come up with this whole personality of what we wanted our dog to be. We talked about how she would be riding in the car with us and all that. We laughed because we were saying how we're going to get this dog and she isn't going to be able to live up to the expectations we set for her.

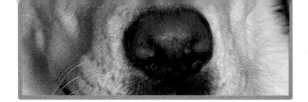

"But actually, Misty does pretty much everything we thought. She's just a great dog.

"As for my racing and me, Misty makes it a lot easier. When you spend the majority of races in your NASCAR career as a go-or-go-homer, you need something to take the stress off. She makes it easier to go back to the bus because she doesn't care if you make the race or if you win. She just wants to play and be fed. She doesn't care. She'll come up to me, lick my face, and want to play. I haven't missed a race since we got her. Good luck? Yeah, maybe she is."

As told by AJ Allmendinger

"Misty is the best thing we could have done for us. I think she was the best thing we could have done for AJ's racing off the racetrack. It gave him something that wasn't all about racing. During the top 35 issue when AJ had to qualify for the race, he would come back to the bus and, whether it was good or bad, he would go and snuggle up with the puppy. And that made a world of difference. Whether he will admit it or not, that made him a happier person at the racetrack and he was easier to deal with."

As told by Lynne Allmendinger 🐾

"*Good luck?*
*Yeah, maybe she is.***"**

AJ with wife Lynne
and dog Misty

Aric Almirola
Ali and Zoe

"**M**y first pet growing up was a Doberman. His name was Magnum. He was cool.

"We lived on a little piece of property, and I had a little playground out in the front of our house. That's where my swing set was, and his dog house was there, too. Right in front of his dog house was a dirt pit. I used to take my matchbox cars and go out there and play in that dirt pit.

"You see, my grandfather raced dirt sprint cars so I always thought that racetracks were dirt tracks. When I was little I didn't even know that there were asphalt racetracks.

"I would go out to the dirt pit, take my matchbox cars and I would race them around. Magnum would watch what I would do with the race cars. He would watch that I would push my race cars around in the dirt. So he would take his nose and he would put it on the back of the cars and push it in the dirt, too. He was such a cool dog.

"He was extremely protective of my family and me. He would play and play with me, but he knew when I was somewhere I shouldn't be and he would growl at me.

"Magnum would never cross the road. If I went out and crossed the road, he would growl at me all the way up until I crossed the road and then, when I would cross the road, he would just start barking at me as loud as he could. That would usually make my mom come out of the house and yell at me.

"Back then, I thought Magnum was a tattle tale, but I know he was just protecting me.

"Because I had such a great dog in Magnum and the other pets I had growing up, I knew that I wanted a pet. When we started looking for a pet, I knew I couldn't have a dog because at that point, I was truck racing. I couldn't take him on the road with me, and I didn't want to take my dog to a kennel every weekend when I went racing.

"So, Janice and I went to Pet Smart one night and looked at cats. It wasn't the first time we had looked. We had been several times. They keep cats in there from the Iredell Humane Society. That night, this cool Calico cat was sitting in there, and we got her. We named her Ali.

"Ali is three-years-old. She's a weird cat, but she's a lot of fun. It's just fun to see her personality. She runs and hides at first when most people walk in. But she loves attention and loves to be out. She wants to be the center of attention. She wants everybody to pay attention to her and pet her.

"A few months ago, Janice thought it would be a good idea for Ali to have a sister because Ali was getting a little overweight and lazy. She thought another cat would keep her active, so that's how we ended up with Zoe.

"Zoe's a kitten. She is about eight-months-old and a lot of fun. She picks on Ali and Ali bosses her around.

"Ali was the queen of the castle, so when we brought Zoe in, she wasn't really happy at first. Zoe

Above: Zoe

Right: Ali

Left: Aric with Janice Goss and cat Ali

would be checking the house out and Ali would be following Zoe wherever she was going. As soon as Zoe would notice Ali, you could see Ali's demeanor go from inquisitive to 'don't get near me.' Ali would just kind of stand-off to Zoe and hiss at her. There were a couple of days of hissing and growling but after a week they were fine.

"Now they run around and chase each other. They lay on the couch together. They've got a funny routine – if one of them wants to play, they'll find the other one and they do that little chirping noise and take off. They'll run up the stairs and through the office and back down.

"I wasn't sure about having two cats, but two is good. It's twice as much cat hair and twice as much cleaning of the litter box, but it really is twice as much fun.

"I'm really glad that we adopted both Ali and Zoe and have given them a home. There's just something about adopting a pet that almost makes you feel better about getting that pet. You've taken an animal that's been tossed outside and unwanted and found somewhere or is hurting. You've taken an animal and you have given it a home where it was living in a two foot by three foot box up until that point.

"There's a small sense of joy in that to give an animal a home that has either had one that didn't want it or has never had one. It really makes you feel good, and it's amazing how much they love you."

Marcos Ambrose
Shelter Dog Dora

"**B**eing from Launceston, Tasmania, Australia a lot of people think I had a pet kangaroo growing up. I joke around and tell people that I did, and that I used to ride in its pouch to school when I was a little boy. But, in all honesty, my pets have been cats and dogs.

"I had my very first dog when I was four-years-old, and her name was Brandy. She was a beautiful Golden Retriever. I just loved her because she was friendly, eager, and energetic. She was the perfect pet because I loved the outdoors and so did she. She was reliable, a good friend, and just a joy to have as a little kid.

"Recently here in America, I was living alone for some time while my wife Sonja and children – Tabitha and Adelaide – stayed back with our family in Tasmania for a few months.

"It got lonely being home all the time by myself, and I really missed my girls. One day, Tad and Jodi Geschickter, who own JTG-Daugherty Racing along with Brad Daugherty, the race team I drive for, asked me if I would be open to fostering a dog until they could find a home for him. They knew I was by myself, and they thought a dog would be good company for me.

"I thought it was a good idea too, and that's how I ended up with Max. Max was small, only about 15 pounds. He was a Jack Russell Terrier mix. He was living in a chicken coop when he was rescued and became an Animal Adoption League foster dog.

"Max and I had a great relationship. We played together. He even enjoyed a bit of freedom with me, but one time a little too much. I let him off his leash, which I learned the hard way you should never do. Of course, he ran away.

"Thank goodness I was able to catch him. One day I called Jodi. She was silent on the other end of the line – I think she thought I had lost Max because I have a history of losing things.

"Instead, I told her that Max was doing okay and that he really enjoyed treats, especially the ones from Starbucks that I was giving him.

"You see, his favorite food was banana nut bread and his favorite drink was cappuccinos. I got in big trouble with Jodi because she told me I was not supposed to give Max anything with caffeine in it.

"Max was really a good distraction for me. He provided an endless amount of comfort and entertainment while I was on my own living in America, and I'm really lucky that I had him. He really was a man's best friend."

About Marcos' shelter dog: Dora is a four-year-old mixed terrier from Noah's Ark in Locust Grove, GA. Dora loves children and other pets.

Michael Annett
Paisley

"**P**aisley is named after country music artist Brad Paisley. He's one of my favorite singers. I ended up getting Paisley not too long after I had seen Brad Paisley in concert for the fifth time, so it seemed like a fitting name.

"Paisley is a two-year-old mini Golden-Doodle, which is a cross between a Golden Retriever and a Poodle. She has blonde curls all over. She's really a cute dog.

"Paisley definitely has her own personality. She has this one toy that is her favorite out of all the bones and toys that she has. She plays with it all the time. But what's funnier than that is she yodels to this toy. She really tries to sing to this toy and yodels just as loud as she can. You can't help but laugh. So when I have people over, I always try to get her to play with that toy. I guess naming her after a country singer was perfect.

"I really think that Paisley thinks she's a cat sometimes, too. At the house, she'll sit on the very top of the loveseat and watch everything that is going on around her. She doesn't want to miss anything. And she always wants to sit on my lap. Like I said, she thinks she's a cat or smaller than what she is. But she always sits on my lap when we're traveling to the races. She wouldn't have it any other way.

"Paisley's a great companion for me. I really can't imagine not having a pet around me. I grew up with pets. I had rabbits, ferrets, dogs, horses, and even a lizard.

"My Golden Retriever Sammi, was probably my favorite pet growing up. She went everywhere with us. I remember this one time, we were at a hotel and Sammi jumped into the hotel pool. I think we all got in trouble for that one.

"To me, it's so important for pet owners to take care of their pets and future pets by having their cat or dog spayed or neutered. By controlling the pet population and preventing the birth of unwanted pets, we are improving the welfare for all animals." 🐾

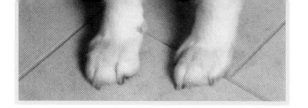

Wayne Auton
Hazel and Dakota

I think I was in eighth grade when my grandfather passed away. When he died, we "inherited" his Bulldog – Trigger.

"Trigger was probably the most loyal dog ever, and he was so protective of me. That dog would sleep outside my room every single night. Each morning, when I would walk to the bus stop, he would walk right beside me. And in the afternoon, when I came home from school and got off the bus, Trigger would be there to walk me back home.

"I guess Trigger was just making sure that I wouldn't get into any trouble, and he was taking good care of me, too.

"The funniest thing about Trigger was his howl. Every once in a while he would start howling, and it sounded just like a siren. Trigger probably lived to be about 15 years or so. We also had Cocker Spaniels when I was a kid, but Trigger was definitely a special dog to me.

"Although I always had a dog growing up, I don't have a pet right now. I'm on the road all the time with the NASCAR Camping World Truck Series, so I would never get to see my pets if I did have one.

"Dakota and Hazel are my "grand-dogs." They are my daughters' Siberian Huskies. Dakota is Tasha's 9-year-old silver Siberian Husky. Hazel is Talesa's 2-year-old red Siberian Husky.

"Dakota was the runt of his litter. He knows how to say please for his food, and he sings. When

he sings, he sounds just like the phone when it rings. It's pretty entertaining.

"Talesa adopted Hazel from the Florida Siberian Husky Rescue. Hazel was found abandoned in a flea market in Gainesville, Florida. Hazel is definitely a handful. We have to watch after her because she's quite the escape artist. She can climb out of anything, and when she does, she is ready to go.

"My wife Libby and I are lucky to have our "grand-dogs" in our life. Although we don't have our own pet, we get to enjoy the companionship and entertainment that a pet gives you through Dakota and Hazel. We have a lot of fun with them when we do get to see them."

Wayne pictured with wife Libby, daughters Tasha and Talesa, and dogs Dakota and Hazel

Although we don't have our own pet, we get to enjoy the companionship and entertainment that a pet gives you through Dakota and Hazel. We have a lot of fun with them when we do get to see them.

Buddy Baker
Bushay and Max Lightning

"**I** had a Russian Wolf Hound when I was a little boy. I think I was about seven when I got Tye.

"Tye loved kids as much as we loved him. He was big enough for me to ride around like a horse. He liked to play football. He was just the best companion, and he really protected me. It's funny actually. I remember one time when I was going to get spanked, Tye starting getting mad and was growling, and I never got that spanking. He protected me. He really was a best friend.

"We rescued both of the dogs we have now because that is something we feel very strongly about. We want to do everything we can to prevent unwanted and homeless animals, so that's why we chose to adopt our pets. I know my wife Shayne has always said she didn't understand how someone could love an animal so much and then just abandon it, and I agree with her.

"We got Bushay from Four Paws Rescue. He's an Australian Shepherd mix, who was a twin in a litter of 14 puppies. Bushay is pretty athletic – he will jump a four-foot high fence. He's also a protector – he stands guard at the koi pond to protect it from the big birds.

"Max Lightning just kind of took up residence at our house one day. He's known as the neighborhood dog, but he sleeps at our house. Max's original owners weren't very responsible. They would just throw food outside for him, and they never gave him any attention. He's a beautiful Retriever mix with long orange hair, and all he wanted was for someone to love him. Max is a super fast dog. Like I said, all he wanted was a little attention, so he walks with me every morning to go get the newspaper, and then he sits down and waits for breakfast.

"If you are a responsible pet owner, I really think the first thing you need to take care of is getting your pet spayed or neutered. That will help keep animals from being homeless or getting euthanized, and it is something everyone should feel strongly about.

"We love all animals, and I have been very lucky to have had some great pets. They love you unconditionally, and that's something that can never be taken for granted." 🐾

Left: Buddy with dog Bushay

Right: Max Lightning

T.J. Bell
Kingston and Richie

"I've had pets ever since I can remember. We had a German Shepherd when I was really little.

"Jethro was a cool dog – just laid back. We had him until I was eight or nine years old, and when he passed away, it took us a while to get another dog. That's how much he meant to us.

"Do you remember those Fisher Price scissors that you buy kids that aren't supposed to be able to cut anything? Well, I guess my mom heard me in the back room saying 'Be still, you're going to look so good.' She came back there, and I had cut off all our German Shepherd's whiskers, and he sat there and let me do it.

"Now, I have an English Bulldog, Kingston, and a Chihuahua, Richie. Kingston is two and weighs 48 pounds. Richie is three and only weighs three-and-a-half-pounds.

"Kingston does not like getting up in the mornings. He will be in bed until 10 o'clock a.m. no matter what anybody else in the house does. In fact, I can get up and take Richie out to go to the bathroom, and I still cannot get Kingston out of the bed.

"But when he does finally wake up, Kingston runs wide open until he goes back to sleep. He is the most active English Bulldog I have ever seen, and he is a pretty smart dog. We have a kiddie pool in the yard because he gets so hot during the summer. We'll put the hose in the pool and run the water. And normally, Kingston just jumps in, bites the hose and starts slinging water everywhere. It's so funny.

"Richie will just stand around and try to drink out of the kiddie pool and bark at Kingston while he is slinging the hose around.

"Recently, Kingston figured out that he can go over, grab the hose, and pull it off the reel and out into the backyard. The hose has gotten shorter and shorter every month because he chews through it. If you walk outside, he will run over to where you turn the hose on and stand there and bark at it until you turn it on.

"Kingston and Richie are pretty good together. They'll play together, and Richie will even clean Kingston's folds.

"They are both kennel trained, which helps when we travel with them to the racetrack or even back home to Reno, Nevada, during the off-season. I know some people think kennel training is mean, but I think it's the best thing because they have their own home no matter where they are.

T.J. with dog Kingston

"You know how every kid always made that little spot where they went to hide? That's kind of like what it is for dogs. It's their safe zone. If they don't like what's going on in the house or their surroundings at that moment, they'll just go lay in their kennel. We leave the TV on next to the kennel and that's their little happy place.

"Giving dogs a happy place is something really dear to my heart. In the past, I ran a special decal on my truck in the NASCAR Camping World Series for 'Home 4 The Holidays' (www. home4the holidays.org), which is an initiative by the Helen Woodward Animal Center in Rancho Santa Fe, California. The goal is to find homes for 1.5 million pets. It's something I feel very strongly about.

"I've donated to their auction, and I've worked to bring attention to them through my racing. Every winter when I go home, I go down to our local animal shelter and I'll put up money for whatever they need to reach their goal for adoptions for the Home 4 the Holidays program.

"That way, whenever people come in to get their pets, they fill out their paperwork like they have to pay the initial fees for the animal, but they really don't. They get the pet for free because I've already put up the money.

" I just think if people don't have the money to buy a pet but are responsible enough to get a pet, they definitely should adopt and I'm going to help them if I can. There are a lot of animals out there that are deserving of great homes." 🐾

T.J. with dog Richie

T.J. with Alexis Gamboa and dogs Kingston and Richie

66*Giving dogs a happy place is something really dear to my heart.*99

Dick Berggren
Indy

"**O**ur dog is by far the most important person in our lives and whatever the dog needs, whatever you think the dog might want, then there you go – that's what we do. It's been that way since we got our first dog.

"Indy is our fourth Airedale. We had lost three, and when the third one passed away, we were devastated. We said we're never going to have another dog. Well, guess what – life is just not the same without one.

"What really did it was one of my really close friends Lou Boyd said to me one day, 'Berggie, where have you been walking lately?' and I said, 'We don't walk anymore, we don't have the dog.' He looked at me and he said, 'You're missing a lot of life.' And I said, 'You're right. You're absolutely right.'

"What really happened to us with dogs was that we had been married for about a year with a parakeet, and that was just a so-so pet. For whatever reason one day, I walked into a pet shop in Sommerville, Massachusetts.

"This little dog raised up on the edge of the cage that it was in. I asked the guy at the pet store, 'Is this going to be a small dog?' He told me yes that all their dogs were small dogs. Here we were, in the middle of a city (Boston) – and who would want a large dog there. I found out later that the pet shop clerk said the dog would be small, but he didn't know.

"The dog was an Airedale mix, and we just loved that dog. I was a psychology student at the time at Tufts University, so I named the dog Freud, which was really funny. When I was teaching class I would say, 'Ladies and gentlemen, this is psychology 101 and Freud has just walked into the room.' That was cool.

"Freud lived to be 14 years old and we had a great time. We had a boat, and she'd go out on the boat. She went to work with me every day. She would walk to school with me. It was really neat. Literally, I would walk into class with that dog.

"When I finally finished school, I got my degree and went to work as a college professor. I took the dog with me. This was an all women's Catholic college as stuffy as they come, and yet, that dog was tolerated by the nuns, by the students, by the priests, by everybody.

"And then, unfortunately, she contracted cancer and we lost her. Two years of grieving

later, along came another Airedale, and this time it was my wife Kathy's turn to name the dog. My wife was a librarian, so that dog was Dewey Decimal. It was really the same sort of thing.

Again, the dog went everywhere with me. But, by the time Dewey Decimal came along, I was racing. There were a lot of times when it was the dog and me in the truck and that was it. We'd go off and race on Saturday night and the races would end and the dog would be under the grandstand picking up hot dogs and whatever else.

"Unfortunately, we lost Dewey at 14 years, also to cancer.

"Another two years of grieving and then along came Joy. And Joy was a joy. Joy was the biggest Airedale we had gotten and she contracted cancer at age six. We lost her that year.

"We weren't going to get another dog, but, like I said, life just wasn't the same. So we decided to go looking for another dog. This dog came from Ohio. I looked for months literally trying to find an Airedale in the Boston area and couldn't find one. My sister went all the way to Ohio to get her.

"It was my turn to name the dog, so I named her after a racetrack, naturally. Indy is a high speed Airedale. Although Indy could also stand for independent with this dog.

"Indy's been around us long enough now that she is so tuned in to our habits and what we do. She's the alarm clock. Every day she gets us up. She tells us when it's time, usually right about dawn, which isn't so bad in February, but right now dawn is at 5 a.m. She wants us up at 5. And when it gets time for lunch she's ready to tell us it's time for lunch. Then it's time for her walk in the woods in the afternoon at 2 o'clock, and she lets me know it is 2 o'clock. At 5 o'clock it's time for supper and then on and on it goes.

"She just knocks me out sometimes. Watching the dog with her head sticking through the pickets of the fence just makes me smile. She has her head through the pickets and she is looking at the boats coming and going and people on the street.

"All of our dogs have always been dogs that we have had around us. We've never had a dog where we would close the door in the morning, go to work, and come back again at night. They always went to work. They always were around a lot of people. They always enjoyed other dogs. They always played with other dogs, had fun with other dogs.

"The dogs make us a family.

"But there are too many animals that don't have homes. For an animal to have a home like this one or the kind of home the Newmans give theirs, that is what every animal ought to have. It doesn't always happen. Spaying and neutering helps that problem. 🐾

"The dogs make us a family."

Dick pictured with wife
Kathy and dog Indy

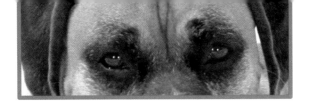

Greg Biffle
Foster, Gracie, and Savannah

"**I** have had a lot of dogs and I have a lot of memories of them, but I had this one dog and what he did was just unbelievable. RC was a Black Lab I had back in Washington. He liked to wander. I would see him down at the stop sign up the hill from our house, and I would get him in the car and then bring him home.

"Well, one day my brother moved out and rented a house with some of his friends that had a fenced yard. He decided he was going to take RC with him. My brother had the dog over there for a couple of weeks, and RC ended up missing, but we didn't know it.

"I was down the road one night coming home, and there was RC. I picked him up and brought him to the house, and I just kind of figured that my brother must have brought him back, so I didn't say anything until the next day when my brother called and said RC was missing from his house.

"And this is no joke. That dog had to cross a six-lane interstate. He had to go over an overpass and a four-lane road with a turn lane. The area wasn't rural, it was completely developed and busy. He went a long way. I still can't believe it. I mean, how did that dog find his way? But dogs just have that sense – they know home. It was amazing.

"Dogs have always been an important part of my life. Now we have Foster, who's the king. He's eight years old. We have Gracie, who is five years old, and Savannah, our rescue dog who is three years old.

"Foster is like the professor. He's the intelligent one. You can always tell what he's thinking. He's just got that attitude. If he's mad at you, he will turn around and lay down with his head pointing away from you. He pouts if you aren't paying attention to him.

"Foster knows when you are packing a bag. He'll block the doorway of the bedroom. He'll just lie down right there. As you get the bag packed, you have to step over him. Then he'll go downstairs and sit in front of the door like 'You're not leaving me. I'm going.' It's funny.

"He got sick last October (2008). He was diagnosed with thyroid carcinoma. They removed the tumor, and he's had a clean bill of health since, but his energy level is reduced a little bit.

"Gracie is like Aqua Dog. It's amazing how much she swims. At first, Gracie would not get her

Greg with wife Nicole, and dogs Gracie, Savannah, and Foster

> *❝I mean, how did that dog find his way? But dogs just have that sense – they know home. It was amazing.❞*

paws wet, but now she just swims all the time. She still doesn't swim very well. She gets into the water and her front legs just slap the water and it splashes like three feet high, but she loves it.

"Savannah is a swimmer, too. She'll chase around the pool cleaner. Savannah chases anything around, and she just loves people.

"We got Savannah when she was about a year old. She had been abused. She has a burn mark on her foot, which the vet said it was a chemical burn. And we think she had been kicked because she is very sensitive around the stomach.

"Helping rescue groups is really where our heart is. We do what we can to help these rescue groups and to get animals like Savannah placed. A lot of people who work with these rescue groups do it for free. Most of them are volunteers, and they are passionate about animals just like we are, so through the Greg Biffle Foundation, we try to give money to a lot of these groups.

"We just try to get our message out. We support the rescue groups, and the biggest thing we try to promote is to spay and neuter your pet. If you can get people to do that, then the shelter and adoption comes second.

"The fans have been so great to support our sport and our Foundations and what we love. A lot of the fans have pets and so that's a neat way we connect to them. They don't have to donate any money or time, but they can still help us with the overall mission. They can be part of the Ryan Newman Foundation or the Greg Biffle Foundation by helping and doing the right thing – by being responsible pet owners or by helping somebody else be responsible." 🐾

Clint Bowyer
Tripp

"**W**hen I was just a kid, I started racing motocross. We traveled all over the Midwest so I could race. And when we would travel, our dog Snapper went with us. Snapper was just a mutt, but because he was always with us, pretty much everyone who raced with us on the weekends knew who he was and who he belonged to.

"Snapper was at the track so often that once when we were at the Ponca City Amateur Nationals in Oklahoma the track announcers made an announcement over the PA system saying that all dogs needed to be on a leash – except for the Bowyer dog. No questions asked. Just thinking about that still makes me laugh.

"I have missed not having the companionship of a dog, so I decided to start looking for one a few months back that would be able to travel with me. That's how I ended up with Tripp.

"Tripp's an Australian shepherd. I found him on the internet the week before the Atlanta race in March, and it just so happened that he was at a breeder who was only about an hour away from the track. We went to the breeder's that Friday morning, and I fell in love with him right away. We took him that weekend.

"Tripp's a puppy so he keeps me on my toes. Every morning, he wakes me up around 7:30 a.m. and from the minute he gets up, he demands attention. If we're at home, I will get up and go outside and walk around the property with him. He likes to play fetch, and if it is hot outside – there is no getting him out of the pool. He just wants to hang out in there.

"He has successfully destroyed every toy that I have given to him since the day I got him. I think I have bought every toy at every pet store around. They all ended up being eaten or in the trash. Here I spent all this money on toys for Tripp, and I found out one day by accident, that all Tripp needs to stay occupied is an empty water bottle. He will play for hours with that.

"When we aren't hanging out at the house, Tripp loves going to the race shop with me. I think he likes all the action there, and I know he loves all the attention. He's been on several recent photo shoots with me, and he is quite the hit. I think he gets more attention than me, which he loves.

"We have a lot of fun. Most weekends, Tripp goes to the track with me. As soon as he is out of the door of the motor home, he is on the golf cart waiting for a ride, and it isn't always my golf cart that he will run and get on. He just likes to ride, and he will try to bum a ride with anyone that he can.

"He definitely makes us laugh. I don't think I could have named him any better because he has been a "trip" ever since I got him."

Colin Braun
Shelter Dogs Danni and Sully

"**I** had two Chocolate Labs growing up – Argo and Spice. They were named after race cars. Argo and Spice were big time competing sports cars back then. We had a cat named Munchkin, too, which was a Midget chassis, but that was my mom's cat. I was much closer to Argo and Spice.

"My parents got them when I was six months old, and had them when I was growing up. We lived on one hundred acres in the middle of Texas, and the dogs loved it. They would go running and exploring for hours on end before they would come back home. They'd return home with deer bones and all kinds of crazy things. You name it, they'd bring it back.

"I remember they came home once with porcupine quills all over their noses. They came back wagging their tails. If you hadn't seen the quills you would have thought that everything was normal. But they had a hundred quills stuck in their tongues and noses, just everywhere. We had to take them to the vet because they have to be removed carefully.

"For me, the dogs are just part of all the memories I had growing up. It seemed like everything I did outside, the Labs, both of them, were always right there.

"My brother and I would play basketball and they would be sitting right there. We'd go exploring around our land and walk around for three or four hours. A lot of the property was wooded and had hills, and we would go everywhere. Argo and Spice would stay right by us. They were awesome.

"I had a bull's wagon I was restoring when I was a little kid. I started working on it when I was nine with my dad. Both the dogs would sit there the entire time. We'd be out there for nine hours a day and they would be lying right there, just watching, just hanging out.

"It's just so cool what dogs add to our lives. They are such a part of the family. All they want to do is be a part of it and know what's going on.

"I miss having a dog. Right now, I have a Beta fish that my girlfriend gave me for Christmas. He's blue and I named him Conway, after my sponsor. I'd never had a fish before. Fish are so easy to take care of. You just have to throw them some food, give them a seven-day feeding block and they're good to go.

"One day, I know I will get another dog. I would love to have a Lab again, they are just awesome dogs. Where I live now, having a third of an acre really wouldn't be fair for the dog. I'm waiting until I have enough property so I can get a Lab." 🐾

About Colin's dogs: Sully (right), an eight-year-old Beagle mix, teaches NC school children how to behave safely around dogs. Danni, a two-year-old German Shepherd mix, is in training to help Sully with the teaching programs.

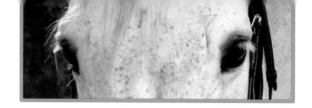

Jeff Burton
Hunter, Lily, Tiger, Andiamo, and Calimero

"**O**ur animals are part of our lives. I love them all, but I don't know that I would have quite so many if it weren't for what it means to Kim, Paige, and Harrison.

"We are loaded up on animals, and it's a lot of work. Kim spends a lot of time cleaning cages and taking animals to the vets. We have cats, dogs, crabs, and a tortoise. And then we have the horses. The horse barn itself takes a lot of time.

"But we all agree that it's worth it.

"Hunter is our Australian Shepherd, and he's six. We got Hunter because Paige wanted a dog, and she wanted the family to have a dog. We got Hunter when he was a little older, so we never really had a puppy.

"Recently, the kids wanted a puppy and Kim wanted a puppy and the more I looked, the more I wanted a puppy, too. We all decided collectively that a puppy would be fun.

"Hunter has been such a good dog that we decided we wanted another Aussie, but we wanted a little smaller dog. That's how we chose the breed – a mini-Australian Shepherd. An Australian Shepherd is the perfect family dog. It's just an incredible dog, real smart, not a mean bone in their body and

kids can play with him all the time. So, we got Lily in the spring.

"A lot of times kids want things without really understanding the responsibility of it. With Lily it was made very clear from the beginning, that if we did get a puppy, they were going to be responsible for cleaning up the puppy's messes, for feeding her, and for taking her out on walks.

"They play with the animals, that's not a problem. They play with them all the time, but we wanted to make sure they took part in all the other stuff. It was explained, in no uncertain terms, that both Paige, 13, and Harrison, 8, would help. And they have.

"It's been really good having the animals. It's taught a lot of lessons about life and death and responsibility.

"We have this one cat – Tiger, who is a gray tabby cat. We found Tiger last winter out in the garage. Paige immediately wanted to keep him. We ended up putting up posters all over – 'kitten found.' And of course, nobody claimed him.

Left: Jeff pictured with dogs Hunter and Lily

Right: Tiger

"We took him to the vet and found out that he had leukemia. So, now we have a cat that stays inside. The kids spend a lot of time with Tiger. Paige has actually taught Tiger to do tricks. He can rear, he can sit, he can fetch, and he can come. She's spent a lot of time with Tiger. At night, you know where to find Tiger – he's with Paige in the bed.

"Our animals have brought more into our lives than we probably realize. Honestly, the time that Paige and Kim have spent together around the horses is irreplaceable. They have spent an incredible amount of time together, cheering for each other, helping each other, and disagreeing from time to time. It's been a great experience for them.

"Our animals are part of our lives. They have brought a lot of joy, a lot of happiness, some disappointments, and some lessons taught for all of us. It's been a really good experience." 🐾

Above: Paige and Harrison with dogs Lily and Hunter

Right: Harrison on horse Calimero

Jeff pictured with wife Kim, daughter Paige, son Harrison, dogs Hunter and Lily, and horses Calimero and Andiamo

❝*It's been really good having the animals. It's taught a lot of lessons about life and death and responsibility.*❞

Kurt Busch
Ginger, Lola, and CJ

"**I**'ve been a Terrier guy my whole life. I had West Highland Terriers growing up.

"I like their attitude and their spunk. Terriers are loving and caring dogs, and, at the same time, they can be tough and mean and have their own attitude.

"Ginger and Lola go to probably 99% of the races with us. It's pretty funny. They know when we are packing the suitcase to leave. They look for their doggie bags, then they willingly jump in and are ready to go.

"Ginger and Lola are our girls, and to us, having them is the same level of responsibility as if we were taking care of our children. The companionship and the sense of family when we are at the track is very cool. It's great to go for evening walks with the dogs.

"When we're at home, I take Lola to the farm – we have some land and I have a little garage out there. She goes with me and turns into a shop dog for the afternoon.

"Ginger just likes to be Miss Independent and roam around on her own. There will be times when we can't find her, and she will be upstairs in one of the bedrooms just lying on top of the bed.

"She's kind of the boss of the house. In fact, she's a little jealous of Eva's new 'child,' CJ, who is an Arabian horse. It's really kind of funny. It seems that, in our family, the lighter you are, the more of the boss ranking that you have.

"So, Ginger's in charge, Lola is next, then Eva. Then it's me and CJ. So we all answer to Ginger – she doesn't care how little she is or how big you are, she's the boss.

"We got CJ, a dapple grey Arabian horse, last summer. Eva grew up with Arabians and grew up riding horses, and she wanted a horse.

"It's been a great thing for Eva. It's a hobby for her, and a release from everyday stress. Just to see her smile and her ability to let everything go, come out to the barn, and enjoy herself is something that you can't beat.

"I'm real proud of her for how she has advanced her riding skills and her attitude with CJ, how she has learned to discipline and guide him. Her motherly instincts with CJ are great to watch. She comes home from the barn happy everyday.

"And that's the thing about having animals, whether it's horses, dogs, or whatever. I think everybody benefits from having an animal. They brighten your day and share their love.

"It's nice to have something to come home to – even at the motor home. You go off, run some errands, and come in to find there is always somebody to greet you. There is always somebody happy to see you.

"They don't care what type of day you had. If you've just slammed your car into the wall going 200 mph and had an awful day, they are still there with their unconditional love saying, "love me.""

Kurt pictured with wife Eva, dogs Ginger and Lola, and horse, CJ

Kyle Busch
Kelly and Suzie

"**W**e always grew up with pets. In our family, we typically had some dog from the Terrier family – Westies, Yorkshires, Cairns. We always had a Terrier of some sort.

"I remember at one point in time I was growing up in Las Vegas, we had Chrissy and Mandy. Chrissy was a Westie and really sweet. Mandy, a Yorkshire, was a little ankle biter.

"So, when I decided I wanted my own dog, I decided to get Westies. Kelly came first and then Suzie.

"Kelly has decided she wants to be an Olympic swimmer. When you throw a flip-flop – just a regular flip-flop in the pool – she'll go and retrieve it for us. She can't get the ball thing down because she can't get it in her mouth unless it's small enough. So she'll grab a flip-flop and bring it back to you. It's pretty funny.

"Kelly and Suzie are always on the road with us. There are a few times when they don't go with us, and when that happens, they go to my Grandma's house for Doggie Day Care. When they go there, it's a full household because there are normally seven Terriers there. Grandma has two, my brother Kurt's two dogs stay there, and my mom and dad's dog stays there, too.

"Most of the time, they are traveling with us, so they are on the go all the time. They get to come to the races and spend time in the motor home. I think the coolest thing about taking them to the track is that they really let us know that home is the motor home, too.

"For Sam and I especially, we love having them on the road because we are away from our family and friends so often. Having Kelly and Suzie there just makes us feel more comfortable. Sam has said before, that it's not so lonely with them there.

"The best thing about the dogs is if you have had a bad day at the track, they don't know.

"I think the most important thing for people to remember is to give your animals love and care. One way to do that is to get your pet spayed or neutered. There's just not enough homes or good places and families for all these animals. They all need love." 🐾

Kyle pictured with Samantha Sarcinella, and dogs Kelly and Suzie

Richard Childress
Johnny Cash and Annie Oakley

"**Y**our dog is your best friend. When I'm around the house early in the morning, Johnny Cash will sit outside with me while I'm drinking my coffee and planning my day. Just to have him around and to enjoy that time with him, there's nothing better. They really become part of your family.

"Johnny Cash is a German Shepherd, who was born in the USA. His father is a champion German protection dog from Germany, as well as his mother. He's solid black, just like the 'Man in Black' and that's where he got the name. You don't see that many just solid, coal black German Shepherds like Johnny Cash.

"We've had him about two years now. We had wanted a protection dog that could be a pet to the family, but was more of a protection dog, so that's how we ended up with Johnny.

"He's a very serious protection dog. He does his work very well. If anyone comes around the compound, he lets you know, but he is also a great pet. He likes to play with Judy and me. When you go outside, he wants you to throw with him first thing in the morning. I go out and have my coffee, and I throw his toys. He goes and runs after them.

"Judy's dog is a Maltese, and her name is Annie Oakley. She has run wide open since we first got her. She is very hyper and just loves Judy. They are like one.

"For me, I try to focus my efforts on protecting and preserving the outdoors for our animals and our children. I have two grandchildren, and I want them to be able to enjoy the outdoors just like I did. And I want their children to be able to enjoy the outdoors, too.

"One of the greatest conservationists of all times was Theodore Roosevelt, and he is probably my hero when it comes to the things he accomplished when it comes to conservation. If I've got to pick a hero, he would probably be one of them because of the things he has provided for so many people who aren't hunters but are outdoorsmen. That's why I really enjoy doing the conservation work that I do.

"I also work very close with the Rocky Mountain Elk Foundation. I'm on the board of directors for the Congressional Sportsman Foundation out of Washington D.C., which works on the rights to protect our lands and our hunting heritage, and to protect a lot of things for outdoorsmen.

"I have put one ranch of mine in Montana in the conservation easement with the Rocky Mountain Elk Foundation, so that the land will never be developed. That's the area where the northern Yellowstone Herd comes and spends time. It is sort of a preserve for them.

"From the time I was a kid, I have loved the outdoors. There was nothing like sitting on the hillside up there waiting for a squirrel or looking for a squirrel when you are 11 or 12 years old. I've been able to share a lot of those times with my grandsons Austin and Ty – both of them are big outdoorsmen and we taught them gun safety when they were very, very young. We taught them that, when you do take an animal, you just don't take it to waste it.

"We have taught them conservation, and that's what it is all about – it's conservation if other people can enjoy wildlife and enjoy all the things about the outdoors."

Richard pictured with wife Judy, and dogs Johnny Cash and Annie Oakley

Stacy Compton
Daisy Mae, Freddy, Maggie, Scooby Doo, and Peaches

"We had talked about getting another dog, as if we needed anything else, last year right around Christmas. Vickie had said she would love to have a Boxer. I went by the local pound. I go by there probably way more than I should.

"Anyhow, there was a Boxer over there. This was probably Tuesday, the week of Christmas in 2008. I asked how long they would be open Christmas Eve. She said they would be open half a day. So on Christmas Eve, I had the girls in the car and Vickie and I said, 'let's ride over to the pound and see that boxer.'

"I knew we were going to bring him home. Well, we got over there and it was closed. It was 11:30 a.m., and they were closed. So we went around the back, because they've got the cages where you can see them if they're not inside. And we didn't see him.

"We could see up the hall, and we could see he was playing in the hall with the guy that was feeding him. So we started beating on the door until he finally came. We told him that we wanted to take that Boxer home. He called a lady, she came in and filled out the paperwork, and we brought him home.

"He was scheduled to be put down soon and we gave him a new life on our farm. He was so happy when we got in the car that he went from car seat to car seat kissing the girls. It was so funny.

"The girls named him Freddy. All our horses, cats, dogs, goats, the miniature donkey, rabbits, everything, we let the girls name all of them, so they all have cartoon character names. So he's got a pretty good home now.

"Freddy's probably one of the smartest dogs I've ever seen. He's got a great personality. I told Vickie that I thought he had followed somebody to the school next to the pound, and that's how he ended up there. He is such a good dog. I feel like somebody probably lost him, but he's got a pretty good home now.

"We figured a couple of scenarios – maybe somebody couldn't afford to keep him and dropped him off or he followed somebody there. Regardless, we are glad that we got him.

"So Vickie wanted one Boxer, and we got Freddy but then we ended up with two more – Scooby Doo, who is only a few months old, and Maggie, who is three years old. We got Scooby Doo so that Freddy would have a friend.

"Then, not long after that, Maggie was thrown out of a van in our friends' yard. They couldn't keep her, so we did. Maggie ran away a lot at first, but now she has settled in and has

taken over one of the chairs by our pool.

"We have the three Boxers, Daisy Mae is a Shih Tzu, we have pygmy goats, horses, rabbits, and we have Patches, who is a Ragdoll cat. Olivia, who is four, kept saying that she really missed Miss Kitty, who was our cat that passed away. So we ended up getting Patches for her.

"Vickie had read on a web site that Patches was a non-shedding cat, and we thought that was perfect. I also thought that it was too good to be true, and it was.

"It also said that Ragdoll cats were perfect with children, and he likes the kids but he doesn't put up with anything. If he's in a mood, watch out.

"He's mellowed out some now. But the girls will be walking by, and, for no reason, he will start chasing them. He's like a dog. He'll chase them through the house a little bit and then he will disappear and the kids are fine. He's got a personality of his own.

"We really love all our animals. We have spayed and neutered all of them because there are so many dogs and cats that need homes already. There are plenty of animals out there, which is why we tell everyone to give shelters a chance. Most of our animals are rescues and came from shelters, and they are such blessings.

"All animals want is love and attention." 🐾

Left: Olivia and Isabella with Scooby Doo

Below: Stacy with wife Vickie, dog Daisy Mae, and cat Peaches

Right: Stacy with wife Vickie, daughters Olivia and Isabella, and dogs Daisy Mae, Scooby Doo, Freddie, and Maggie

We really love all our animals. We have spayed and neutered all of them because there are so many dogs and cats that need homes already.

Brad Daugherty
Shelter Dog Mulan

"I'm a farm kid. I grew up with cats, dogs, cows, horses, pigs; you name it, we had them.

"I've always been around animals and loved animals. I'm an outdoorsman. I spend a lot of time camping. Every type of critter or animal out there, I've been in contact with it. So, I've always been interested in doing what I can to help.

"As an adult, I had a German Shepherd which we actually got when he was 2½ years old. His name was Xandor. He was being trained as a protection dog to protect my family when I was away. But that didn't work he actually became the biggest baby you've ever been around in your life.

"But Xandor was pretty amazing. He had a lot of impact on my family. He actually saved my niece's life one time. She fell into our swimming pool when all the adults were away. She was just out there messing around while her grandma was on the phone. Grandma happened to look out and saw the dog. Xandor jumped into the pool and actually got a hold of my niece's little bathing suit and pulled her out of the water.

"He was awesome. That was my buddy. He lived to be about 14½ years old. I lost him last year, and that was really tough.

"I have done a lot of work with the Humane Society of Asheville, North Carolina. We are actually getting ready to open a new animal shelter in Asheville. Myself, along with Andie McDowell, the actress, co-chaired it. It's really been incredible. Ninety-five percent of the money came basically from public donations from our community.

"That's the thing – people love their animals. We had an old facility up in western North Carolina. It was a little run down. People came through and saw the old facility that the animals were in and they wanted to do something.

"We just wanted to give the animals a dignified place to come, to either live out their last days because they are dealing with sickness, or to be there while they are waiting for adoption opportunities. The community stepped up, and it was great.

"We've got a brand-spanking-new facility up there and we are taking care of sick animals. We've got some healthy ones too that want to be adopted. It's really a great place. They do a great job. They try to stay away from euthanasia if they can possibly do that with our animals.

"I also tell people to get involved. Try to be as involved in your Humane Society's programs as possible. It's very important that they receive donations to keep these facilities open and operating because they will not survive without people helping out.

"To me, that's a very important part of having pets that I think people need to participate in." 🐾

About Brad's shelter dog: Mulan is a two-year-old female Black Lab mix. She loves to swim, and to play with children and other pets.

Dale Earnhardt, Jr.
Buffalo Laverne and Shirley, and Longhorns Dance 'Til Dawn, Sl Shadows Tiger Lily, and Sl Lindy Lou

"**W**e grew up on a lake, and I remember spending the summers with our dogs. I loved my dogs and spending time with them. Those were special times. I had several dogs growing up – an Irish Setter named Rocket, a Cocker Spaniel named Dusty, and my dad had a pit bull named Killer.

"That's how my boxer got his name.

"I got Killer from Greg Biffle. He's actually the son of Greg's dog Foster. Greg and Nicole brought Killer to the Indianapolis race in August 2004. I had been looking for a dog, and I fell in love with Killer from the moment I met him. He came home with me from that race.

"Killer's my buddy. He loves to ride in the front seat of the car with me, and he thinks that if I'm going somewhere that he's going to go, too. Most of the time, he's pretty lazy.

"Buddy the cat was my first pet out of the group I have now. I got him in New Hampshire in July 2000. We went to a local mall after a Nationwide race, and my bus driver and I found this little ball of fur. We called him Buddy the first day while we were trying to come up with a name for him, and it just stuck.

"Buddy was my traveling companion for several years, but he stays at home now with his brother Tux. I got Tux at a pet store, too. My sister Kelley and I went to the store to get fish, and I left with this cool looking cat, against my sister's better judgment. Tux is as playful as they come, and he can fetch Q-Tips better than you could teach any dog.

"Last year, I got Stroker – a Great Dane. I named him after the Burt Reynolds movie "Stroker Ace." He already weighs over 100 pounds and he could be a lot bigger still. Stroker is my trouble-maker. It's not that he really gets into trouble – he's just a little mischievous. He likes to sneak around my property and see what all he can get into out there. He's pretty funny actually.

"Stroker definitely lets me know when he wants something. He knows how to get my attention.

"In the past year, I also decided to get some buffalo and Longhorns for my farm property. I guess I wanted something a little different than the traditional farm animals, so I got Laverne and Shirley the buffalo.

"Buffalo are pretty interesting. They get along okay with the three Longhorns most of the time, but they have a tendency to get both temperamental and territorial. They'll roam over to the Longhorns and take over their grazing spot, like they own the pasture.

" My best memories have been the unconditional love I have had for all my pets and they have had for me. "

"We also have to make sure that Laverne and Shirley always get fed before the other animals. If they don't, they get restless and can be aggressive.

"When I'm home and hanging out on the property, I'll give Laverne, Shirley, and the Longhorns carrots and special treats.

"If I've learned anything, it's that pet ownership is a big responsibility with a lot of commitment. So, I would tell everyone, that before you add a pet to your family, think about the obligation.

"When you do add pets to the family, it's a great thing. My best memories have been the unconditional love I have had for all my pets and they have had for me. That's why I donate and try to do my part to help further efforts toward animal well-being and animal rescue." 🐾

Buffalo Laverne and Shirley

Tad Geschickter
Mr. Big Feet

"All of our pets have been rescued in some way or another.

"Pets offer so much and ask for so little in return, and ours have definitely enriched our lives. That's why we do what we can to help. We've worked with Animal Adoption Leagues for the past 15 years, and we have also worked with the Pilots-N-Paws program where we take pets to other areas of the country.

"Right now, we have one dog, one cat, two pot-bellied pigs, and seven foster dogs. Of course, that number changes as we take in more pets to foster as they wait on finding a home.

"Mr. Big Feet, our dog, was rescued from a home that no longer wanted him. That dog would cross the road from his house to our old race shop every single day, and Tad would let him inside the shop. He would sleep under Tad's desk. One day at the shop, an animal control officer stopped by to let us know that he had been called to pick up a stray. It turns out that the people had called animal control on their own pet. We kept him from that day on.

"Big Orange, our cat, just showed up in our driveway one day. I used to have to sneak out to the bushes to put water and food out for him because he would run away. But then one day, the cat walked right up to me and rubbed against my leg. He followed me into the house, and he has been sleeping beside me in bed ever since.

"Then we have our two pot-bellied pigs – Bullet and Beasley. They are both very big boys. Bullet is 300 pounds. He had been returned to a pet store and was no longer wanted. We took him so that he would not be discarded.

"Beasley was a friend's pig, who was moving out of state. She couldn't keep the pig anymore so we made a trade. She actually took one of the dogs I was fostering, and I took Beasley. We visit with each other each year at Texas Motor Speedway.

"Our seven foster dogs – Plato, Little Red, Joey, Teeny, Luke, Opus, and Sparkle – all have different stories. Most of them have been found in different parking lots around the country, and we have taken them in while we try to find them a home.

"That just shows how serious a problem pet overpopulation is. There are literally thousands of pets that are discarded every day, and that's why people need to be educated about the importance of spaying and neutering their animals.

"There are so many pets out there waiting to find a good home like our foster dogs. They deserve a chance at a happy life. I would encourage anyone to adopt a rescued pet. They are some of the best pets out there." 🐾

Tad pictured with wife Jody and dog Mr. Big Feet

Tony Gibson
Harley and Mabel

"**I** had this dog Rex when I was a little boy. He was a little Boxer dog. I was probably around five or six years old then. Rex went everywhere my two brothers and I went.

"We would take him to church camp with us during the summer, on vacation, everywhere. Rex was an awesome soccer player. He would push a soccer ball all day long until his nose was raw and bleeding. He could move a soccer ball. As kids, we would play soccer with the dog, and the dog was much better than we were. Everybody was always amazed by how good Rex could play soccer.

"Rex was probably my favorite pet when I was a kid – I loved them all, but he was probably the closest one to me out of all of them. Now that we're all adults, my brothers and I still have pets.

"We have two Beagles – Harley and Mabel.

"Harley doesn't have a tail, and she has a little Boxer in her. We got her from a man who was raising Beagles to be rabbit hunting dogs. He normally didn't sell them, but we had a friend that knew him. So Beth, my little girl Lainee, and I went over there. Lainee wanted a puppy. The guy let them all out of the cage – there was about 10 of them – and Harley ran straight to her. So Harley was ours from that moment on.

"Mabel was a stray. She just kept hanging around the neighborhood. Nobody knew where she came from. She didn't have tags or anything. She was a well-behaved dog. She had definitely been an inside dog before. We really didn't want her going to the pound, so we took her in, took her to the vet and got all her shots.

"She was in very good health. I guess somebody just set her out. She had been wandering the neighborhood for about a week or so when we finally took her in and adopted her. That was about three years ago, and Mabel's been ours ever since.

"They are hooked at the hip. They go everywhere together. They sleep together. They love one another like little sisters. As close as the two dogs are, they are really different.

"Harley will chase rabbits and birds. We have a bird feeder in the front yard, and Harley will get over in the corner of the yard and she'll hunker down and watch those birds. As soon as the birds get on the feeder, she'll take off running at them. She'll try to jump up there and get the

birds and the birds just tease her. They know she can't get up there to them.

"But all Mabel does is lay around and sleep and eat. Mabel's not much of a runner. She just kind of hangs out.

"They're a huge part of our family. They're just like kids to us. It's amazing how close and attached you get to animals. Like I said, they are one of us. They are part of our family and always will be."

As told by Tony Gibson

"Snoopy is the most famous Beagle and Harley definitely has some of those characteristics. She's the trouble-maker. She's the one that's into everything all the time.

"She has chewed the siding off our house. She thought that was funny. When she was a puppy, she chewed through the wire on the eye-beam light and the garage door wouldn't work anymore.

"I called the garage door opener guy to come fix the eye-beams. He comes and he fixes the eye-beams, and I pay him. He pulls out of the driveway and Harley had already chewed through them again.

"Harley was a mess. She is Tony's dog. Every Sunday night when we get home from the racetrack, she will come outside into the driveway. She will flip over on her back in front of Tony and start talking to him. She will just scream at the top of her lungs until Tony talks to her and pets her.

"This is every Sunday night when we get home from the racetrack, so the neighbors know when we get home. They can hear her screaming and talking to Tony when we get home.

"She is Tony's baby and Mabel is my baby. If she is in the house, she will follow me from room to room to room. If I go into the walk-in closet, she goes into the walk-in closet. She wants to know where I am at all times.

"They really are just like kids. This summer, Lainee was here with the Nanny and Harley got run over accidentally. Harley ended up okay, it just kind of took the skin off of her leg.

" I was a basket case at the racetrack. I was in tears on the pit box. I had Krissie (Newman) in tears on the pit box. They're just part of your family. They're like your kids.

"You want to help them, but you don't know how to help them. It was just the worst weekend ever. You just feel helpless. They are such a big part of your family. "

As told by Beth Gibson 🐾

Tony pictured with wife Beth, daughter Lainee, and dogs Harley and Mabel

> **"They're a huge part of our family. They're just like kids to us. It's amazing how close and attached you get to animals. Like I said, they are one of us. They are part of our family and always will be."**

Darian Grubb
Poppy and Lola

"**I** lived on a farm so we had cows and pigs. The first pets that I remember are two Collies that we named Smokey and Bandit.

"After Smokey and Bandit passed away, we had Chelsea. She had a litter of puppies one time while we were on vacation. We kept one of those puppies and his name was Max, a Black Lab/German Shepherd mix.

"My Dad owned a construction company and Max was the shop dog. He always hung out there, and the guys used to play really rough with him. They would sit there and tease him with crackers, nabs, and stuff at break, then would chase him away.

"He had this really long tongue and would stick it out of his mouth. The guys would actually grab him by his tongue and swing him around. It sounds awful, but he loved it. It was almost like, the rougher you played with him, the more he liked it. He was just a crazy dog.

"Max got run over one time and broke a hip, so he had arthritis that we gave him pills for every day. But he still made his daily trek from the house to the shop. He would stay at the shop all day. He would actually hear Dad's old diesel truck coming up the road from about a mile and a half away and he would go out to the door and sit and wait for dad to pull in with the truck.

"He was a great dog. I think we had him 14 years before we had to put him down.

"We haven't gotten a dog yet, but when Gavin gets old enough to help take care of the dog and appreciate it, we are definitely going to adopt a dog. They say those "Heinz 57s" make the best pets.

"I want to have an outdoor dog because, to me, it seems like they love it and they just thrive in that environment."

As told by Darian Grubb

"Darian didn't have weird animals until he married me. Right now we have Lola, the school bunny and Poppy our Quaker parrot.

"I joke that he didn't realize when he married me that he not only got me, but he got a bird that's like a step-child because that bird will be here forever. Poppy is 13 years old. She will live until she's about 30.

"She is too funny.

"At our house, the fireplace is in front of this big chair and Poppy's cage is behind the chair. We came home one night, and didn't turn the lights on or anything. We just had the fire going. Darian was sitting in the chair, and he told me to come sit with him in the chair. So I kind of just slipped into the chair. Neither of us said anything. We didn't do anything.

"All of a sudden, you hear Poppy go 'hmm-mmm, hmm-mmm.' And then she starts kissing (smacking noises) and going 'hmm-mm.'

"We weren't doing anything and you couldn't see anything except for the fire. But because Poppy saw me get in the chair with Darian, she just thought 'Okay, I know what they are doing.' We just died laughing.

"When she was a baby I would always hug her and go 'Hmm-mm Poppy, I love you.' So when she sees two people showing affection that's what she does. She goes 'hmm-mm,' and then she starts making kissing noises. She's something.

"When the phone rings and you get ready to get off the phone, you don't have to say 'Bye.' You can just say, 'I'll talk to you later' or 'I'm gonna go' and Poppy will say 'bye-bye.'

"Or you can be telling a story and she'll say 'Oh really, oh really?' You can scream at her and scold her when she gets really loud, and if you use a certain voice with her and say 'Poppy', she'll say, 'Stop that squealing, stop that squealing, stop that squealing!'

"So, she's got a big vocabulary of about 60 words or so. She gives kisses. She loves toothpaste. She loves French fries, and she loves corn on the cob. She'll eat corn, and she eats the meat out of the corn, and she gets the corn kernels all over her face.

"She does the same thing with green peas. She loves green peas, but she will take that green pea and she'll eat the meat out of the inside, and then she will have these little seed pockets all over her face of green peas because she loves them. She's definitely entertaining."

As told by Yolanda Grubb

Above: Darian pictured with wife Yolanda, son Gavin, bird Poppy and rabbit Lola

Right: Gavin pictured with Poppy and Lola

Kevin Harvick
Bebe, Endy, and Lo

"I grew up with cats and dogs, but not quite as many as we have now. I've always been kind of a pet person.

"Growing up I had some cool dogs. I had a Beagle named Tippy when I was really young. He would chase a tennis ball until his mouth would bleed. After Tippy, I had a Basset Hound named Lucy that liked to swim. We would come home, and Lucy would actually be lying on a raft floating around the pool. Lucy was probably the coolest dog I had.

"When I moved to North Carolina, I got Mills who is 10 now. Mills is our shop dog at Kevin Harvick, Inc., because she doesn't get along with Bebe. We have to keep them separated because Mills is so old she just gets beat up, so we have to keep them apart.

"Each morning Mills rides with me to the shop. If I'm not at home, somebody will take her for me. And then every night, Mills goes home. She gets fed first, and she hangs out in the backyard. The other dogs hang out in their kennel.

"Endy is nine. He came from Czechoslovakia. He's a German Shepherd that is a fully trained obedience and protection dog. A lot of people think he is named after the race in Indianapolis, but ironically enough, he just happened to come with that name, which is pretty cool. Endy knows all German commands.

"Bebe came from the same breeder as Endy, just obviously a different litter. We got Bebe when she was six months old, and she is seven now. Lo came from Texas, and she is five.

"Lo is probably our funniest dog. She has a big personality. Here she is, all of four-and-a-half or five pounds, and she thinks that she is in charge. She's really mouthy. And when all the dogs come in, she just tries to take control of the house.

"Endy is the exact opposite. He's just really laid back. He doesn't do anything. He just looks at the other dogs like 'I'm bigger than you, leave me alone.' And he'll just lie down.

"Bebe is our hyper dog. She wants to just run and play all the time. She'll jump in the swimming pool. She always wants to be on the go. She's just got to keep going all the time.

DeLana pictured with dog Lo

Kevin pictured with dog Bebe

"Dogs and pets in general are just so cool. They don't care how your day was or if what you did was good or bad, they just know that you're home and hanging out with them.

"For us, we obviously take really good care of our dogs. They go for regular check-ups at the vet. Actually, Lo goes and stays with the vet during the day. She had to have her first and second vertebrae fused back together a while back. During that time, they actually got to know her so well, that she just goes and hangs out at the vet now.

"But all our dogs go for appointments. They have check-ups. They get their teeth cleaned. Our pets are just like us. Since we don't have kids, they pretty much are our children and we treat them like that." 🐾

"They don't care how your day was or if what you did was good or bad. They just know that you're home and hanging out with them."

Kevin pictured with wife DeLana, and dogs Endy, Bebe, and Lo

Rick Hendrick
Diesel and George

"Diesel was Ricky's dog. He loved that dog so much. Now, Diesel lives with us, and he loves Linda. Diesel is a protective little booger. He'll yelp at me if I get too close to her. Each day when Linda retreats to her favorite chair to read, Diesel immediately takes refuge in her lap.

"I have to admit, I instigate a lot with Diesel, too – just to see how protective he truly is. We have a lot of fun with him. He has become a baby to both of us.

"My parrot, George, lived here at home with us for some time until he made his full time residence at Hendrick Motorsports. There's a ton of stories about George.

"I used to take a shower with him in the mornings all the time. When I got up, I would go get him and he'd get into the shower on my shoulder. Then, he'd come with me when I'd go into my closet to put on my clothes for work.

"When I would start putting my socks on, he knew it was time to leave so he would bite my feet. He bit my toe one morning, and I thought he had bit my toe off he had bit it so hard. I kicked him and he rolled about three or four times. He came right back with his wings out, at my feet again. After that, I started putting him back into the cage before I put my socks on.

"I think the funniest thing about him though is he knows he can scare people. He will let them get into a position where they can't really see him before he cuts loose. We have ladies that clean our house and he gets all the way up inside his cage, and doesn't say a word until they are just past him. Then he screams. They jump and run and drop the vacuum cleaner. He gets a charge out of that. People come in and he doesn't say anything until they get right up to the cage and then he screams.

"George would mock the little poodle we had. He would say 'Come here Pebbles, come here Pebbles, and Pebbles would come up looking around. He could imitate a knock on the door, and you would go open the door, and there'd be nobody there.

Diesel

"His cage was beside my desk for so long and I would say 'Yep, yep, yeah buddy, yeah buddy' and he would just sit there at night and imitate me 'Yep, yep, yeah buddy, yeah buddy.'

"One night, one of the guys that worked for us was staying over at the motorsports office in a little apartment, and he heard some people talking. He thought that someone had broken in but it was George in there having a conversation as two different people.

"George will talk in different people's voices, but he won't do it in front of you. You've got to get out of the room, and then he will start it.

"There's just tons of funny stories about George. We all enjoy him." 🐾

Linda with dog Diesel

❝*We have a lot of fun with him. He has become a baby to both of us.***❞**

Above: Diesel

Left: George

Ron Hornaday
Lucy, Elmo, Susie, Muffy, and Brat

"Lindy and I have had a lot of pets. She got me a parrot one time named Buddy.

"He would always bite me at first, but then I became friends with him. He went everywhere with me on my shoulder. If I was in the garage or in the house, Buddy was there with me.

"Lindy taught him how to talk and he knew all these words. He even used to do this rap song. All the guys on my team back then had made a song up for me, and Buddy used to say that. As soon as you would cover up his cage, he'd whisper to you 'good night' and 'I love you.'

"When we'd be working on the cars, Buddy was right there under the hood with us. The only time he would quit working on the car was when we had it fired up.

"Back then, you could take the front end off of the race cars. Buddy would walk across everything, but one time he mistook an exhaust pipe for a roll bar and when he went to walk on it, it was hot and he burned the bottom of his foot. He quit working on cars after that. He just stayed inside the cars and sat in the driver's seat.

"Now, my constant companion is Lucy, our Australian Shepherd. Lucy is funny. She is my dog, but she won't get off the bed until Lindy feeds her each morning. As soon as Lindy feeds her though, she is sitting by the shower until I get out. She'll jump into the truck with me, and she's ready to go wherever I go. She'll mow the grass with me. She'll go swimming with me. She'll do everything.

"No matter what you do in life, when you come home, your dogs don't know why you are mad or sad or anything. They just love you no matter what. You can't find a better friend or a better companion than a dog – other than my wife, of course. It's just so cool."

As told by Ron Hornaday

"My family had animals around us all the time. We didn't usually have that many animals in our house growing up, but we always had animals.

"At one point in time, Ron and I had a blind rabbit, a cockatoo, a parrot, a macaw, a goat, three dogs, two cats, and a pot-bellied pig all living in a 988 square foot house. The goat didn't live in the house, he only came in occasionally with a diaper on. We had a house full, and we loved every minute of it.

"Now, we have four dogs and a cat.

"Ron got Elmo for me for Christmas about 14 years ago. We were watching America's Funniest Home Videos, Ron's favorite show. There was this video with this little Shih Tzu. They were dragging him on the floor, and he looked just like a mop. I was laughing and told

Ron that I thought it was the cutest dog. So, that's what I got for Christmas.

"Then I ended up getting Susie for Ron for Valentine's Day a few months later.

"We took them to races and everywhere with us. We went to Texas one year, and we didn't take the dog. It was when Tony Stewart was racing in the IRL, and he was at the track for the IROC race. Tony was a friend of ours, and he brought his little Shih Tzu, Bud, over and asked us to watch him. It made me miss my dogs so much that I went and found a Shih Tzu the next day in Texas, bought him and named him Stewart after Tony. That dog was just wild. We lost him two years ago.

"Muffy was our daughter Candice's dog. Muffy and Stewart got so attached that when Candice moved out, we kept her dog because they were just so close. Muffy is actually the sweetest dog we have.

"We just kind of ended up with Brat. We had a cat that was pregnant at the house. I came home one night, and my dogs didn't greet me. Well, it turned out that the cat had her kittens in front of my television in the kitchen where my four dogs stayed during the day.

"When I came in, the cat had had the kittens and my dogs were licking them for her. All but one died because they had gotten too far away from the Momma cat and they got cold. The only reason Brat lived was because the Momma cat had just had her. It was so sad to see what happened, but it was the most adorable thing I ever saw because my dogs were trying to help the Momma cat have her kittens.

"All our pets right now are rescues except for Muffy. We just inherited her from our daughter. Our animals are so much a part of our family.

"If people have the opportunity and they are going to get a dog or cat, I hope they go see the shelter animals that need a home. It's sad to see what happens to animals because of the overpopulation and because people don't know how to take care of them. There are just so many animals that need a home, and they turn out to be the sweetest animals."

As told by Lindy Hornaday

Above: Elmo

Right: Lucy

> *"You can't find a better friend or a better companion than a dog – other than my wife, of course."*

Ron pictured with wife Lyndi and dogs, Elmo, Lucy, and Muffy

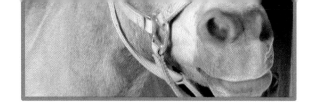

Jay Howard
Emma, Cutter, Teddy, Bert, Lily, and Barney

"I remember having a Beagle when I was younger. His name was Happy. When Happy passed away in an accident, I got another Beagle, and I named him Happy, too.

"My wife Kim grew up with horses, so I think it was inevitable that we were going to end up with horses one day.

"Right now, we have five horses, along with our dogs and cats. The dogs and cats are strays that just showed up at our house, and we have had them spayed and neutered and we take care of them now.

"Cutter is a Buckskin Quarter Horse. We went to Fort Worth for a race, and we ended up bringing Cutter back home. Luke is also a Quarter Horse. He is our trail horse.

"Sherman was a Show Pony. When the little girl who owned him outgrew him, we decided to give him a home. Sherman is our daughter Grace's horse.

"We adopted Emma, our Clydesdale, when she was five months old. They wanted her to have a good home where she wouldn't be used for promotional work, so she became ours. After we got Emma, we decided that she needed a playmate. That's how we ended up with Teddy, our miniature horse.

"It's really amazing because Emma and Teddy bonded from day one. As soon as Teddy sees Emma, he calms down. They are actually so close that we had to cut a mail slot between their stalls so that they could always see each other.

"It's pretty funny when you think about it that Emma and Teddy became so close with Emma being a Clydesdale and Teddy being a miniature horse. The difference between them, when it comes to food intake, is a gallon of milk (Emma) to a shot glass (Teddy), but they don't like to be apart." 🐾

Jay pictured with wife Kim, daughter Grace and son Jay, horses Emma, Cutter, and Teddy, dogs Bert and Lily, and cat Barney

Right: Baby birds found in Jay's barn

Dale Jarrett
Shelter Dog Mia

"**S**ince Kelley and I have been together, we have always had a Siamese cat, at the very least. The kids had a dog – a yellow Lab named Zoe, but we had to put her to sleep a few years ago. So, right now we just have a Siamese cat named Samantha.

"She's gotten old now, but she was pretty rambunctious when she was younger.

"Samantha is such a talker. She is a very loud cat. She lets us know exactly where she is in the house and when she wants to go outside, and of course, you can hear her from the outside when she is ready to come back in.

"When she was younger, you could literally hear her coming through the house from a long way away – she wasn't meowing – you could just hear her running at breakneck speed. I guess she was in the perfect family for that for a really long time.

"Actually, it was pretty funny to watch her. We have some tile floors at our house and she would have difficulty stopping sometimes she was going so fast. She has always been quite the entertainer.

"In Catawba County, North Carolina, where I live, we have a great Humane Society, thanks to the hard work of a lot of people. We had a family friend, Bud Lofland, who had a great heart for animals. He helped a lot of people and animals in this area, so it's something that has stayed important to many of us around here.

"So I think it's important to tell people, that if you want a pet, go to your local Humane Society. They have so many animals, that make great pets. These animals are just looking for a home and somebody to love and take care of them. It's just a great opportunity. And I believe that whatever area you are in – you can find a really good pet for yourself and your children.

"And when you get that pet, just make sure you have them spayed and neutered. That's an important thing to do." 🐾

About Dale's shelter dog: Mia is a Vizsla at the Humane Society of Catawba County. She is one year old and was rescued from animal control. Mia is very sweet and loves kids.

Ned Jarrett
Shelter Dog Gryffindor

"**I** grew up on a farm, and we had lots of animals. "We had a dog named Spot. I don't know what type of dog it was, but I remember that he was not a very large dog. Spot was my favorite out of all the dogs and cats that we had.

"There were six kids in our family, so we all shared the pets. We didn't have one each, but Spot was kind of my dog. That's why he was my favorite.

"Spot was always so friendly. He would just come up to me and play when he might not play with the others. It didn't really matter who was around. It always seemed that Spot would come to me. I liked that attention Spot gave me, so I would always give him some kind of special treat and good things to eat.

"I don't have pets now because of my allergies, but I do remember Spot and the other pets I had growing up. So I know how important pets are.

"A good friend of mine, Bud Lofland, worked really hard to bring attention to Humane Society of Catawba County. After I learned how much Bud was involved in the Humane Society, I began to get more interested in it and appreciated what the Society does as far as pets are concerned.

"People can go there and adopt a pet. They normally have a good variety because the same pet doesn't fit everybody. You can go there and look at the dogs, play with them and do whatever, to get a feel for whether that pet suits you and your family. I really appreciate what he has done there.

"Anyone can adopt a pet there and know that it's clean and okay. People don't have to worry about diseases or anything else. At the Humane Society, the pets are taken care of and are in tip-top shape.

"I'm not sure that everyone realizes that the Humane Society of Catawba County and other Humane Societies offer low-cost spay and neuter programs, and I wish people would. They might take better care of their pets.

"Maybe as time goes by, the things that Bud did and the platform that he set, will help to continually educate people about all the services offered by the Humane Society." 🐾

About Ned's shelter dog: Gryffindor is a Picardy Shepherd/Wolfhound mix. He is three years old and came to the Humane Society of Catawba County (NC) about a year ago. Gryffindor was neglected before his owners were "persuaded" to turn him over. He is very energetic, lovable, and smart. He needs some obedience training, but he has a lot of personality.

Jimmie Johnson
Maya and Roxie

"Maya and Roxie are great companions to us and to each other. They go everywhere with us and luckily are such great travelers.

"We got Roxie first, and it wasn't long after we got her that we decided to get her a sister – Maya.

"They love to play together, and are so entertaining just to watch. They will chase each other all over the house. This summer, we spent a lot of time at the beach, and they would run and run for hours. They both loved running and playing in the sand, but they both hated the water.

"Roxie, our Shih Tzu, is six now. I guess you could call her our social dog. Roxie loves to be right in the middle of all the action. When there are people around, she wants to be right there. She loves when people hold her and fuss over her and just shower her with affection.

"Maya is a Havanese, and she is our guard dog. She's five-years-old. She will sit on the back of the sofa so she can watch everyone and everything that is going on in the house. She's the complete opposite of Roxie around people. You really have to earn Maya's love. She has to know you and trust you before she will show you any affection or even act like you exist.

"Maya and Roxie are such a big part of our lives. We love them like they are our children, and we are so fortunate to have them.

"They've added so much to our lives and brought so much joy to us that we recently got some friends of ours a Golden Retriever puppy from a fundraiser in Charlotte. We knew that the dog would give them so much happiness, so we wanted our friends to have him. I have to admit though, that we almost kept him for ourselves.

"We've enjoyed watching our 'nephew puppy' grow, and we know our friends are enjoying every minute of it.

"Having pets is a lot of responsibility. As soon as we got Maya and Roxie we spayed them. We didn't want to breed them and we didn't want to take any risks with them either. That was something we felt very strongly about, and we knew it was our duty as a pet owner.

"Our pets depend on us to take care of them, and spaying them is just one of the ways we do that. We shower both Maya and Roxie with love and attention, but what they give to us is priceless."

Jimmie pictured with wife Chandra, and dogs Maya and Roxie

Right: Maya

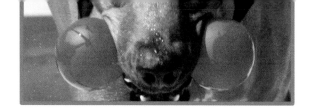

Junior Johnson
Princess, Doodles, and Savage

"**A**nimals have so much to give if we are willing to give to them. They are just one of God's greatest gifts. I mean, truly, they are such a blessing in our lives.

"They need time, love, and attention, and I think the more you give them, the more you will get from them. We've had so many great pets – purebreds and rescues. It doesn't matter. We have loved them all.

"Junior always talks about pets he used to have. He always had dogs from the time he was a kid. He talks a lot about his hunting dogs because when he was growing up they hunted in the mountains for food.

"About 25 years ago, he had a Rhodesian Ridgeback named Savage. Junior just adored that dog. The first Savage – his Savage – really loved Junior and was very protective of him. If you got around Junior, the dog would get between you and him. You really had to pass the dog's inspection first before you could get to Junior.

"Savage was with Junior all the time. Unfortunately, someone left antifreeze out at the race shop, and Savage got into that and died. It really, really hurt Junior. He has always been pained over that.

"So, since Robert was a baby, Junior has told me he wanted to get a Rhodesian Ridgeback for him when he got older. We got the second Savage three years ago. They are the same breed, and they look just alike, but they are natured much differently.

"This Savage has a completely opposite personality than the first one. There's not one aggressive, assertive bone in his whole body. He is the biggest baby you could ever imagine.

"We have Doodles and Princess, too.

"Doodles is a mix of a Chesapeake Bay Retriever and a Lab. We found out last year that she was diabetic. We give her insulin injections twice a day, and she gets a special kind of food every meal. She is doing fabulous, and you would never know the problems she has.

"Princess is the farm dog. She wants to go with Junior everywhere he goes and hang out in the truck. We have to be really cautious in the summertime. Junior doesn't take her at all during the summer because he's afraid he'll close the

Junior pictured with dogs
Savage and Doodles

Above: Princess and Savage

Right: Princess

Junior pictured with wife Lisa, son Robert, daughter Meredith, and dogs Savage and Doodles

door and forget about her. It's just not a good idea to have a pet in the car in the summertime at all. So we just don't let her get into the vehicle in June, July, and August but then she resumes in the wintertime. She takes care of the farm.

"Animals have just been so important to us. We have a home in Atlantic Beach, N.C., and we take Savage and Doodles with us when we go. We just couldn't stand it down there without them.

"Animals just need love more than anything, and they will take whatever you have to give them. The number one way to do that, is encouraging people to help control the pet overpopulation. Spay and neuter your pet, and prevent having unwanted animals. There are so many beautiful animals that have so much to give.

"It doesn't matter what kind of shelter you give them, they just want love and attention. They will be your best friend in the world."

As told by Lisa Johnson 🐾

66Animals just need love more than anything, and they will take whatever you have to give them.99

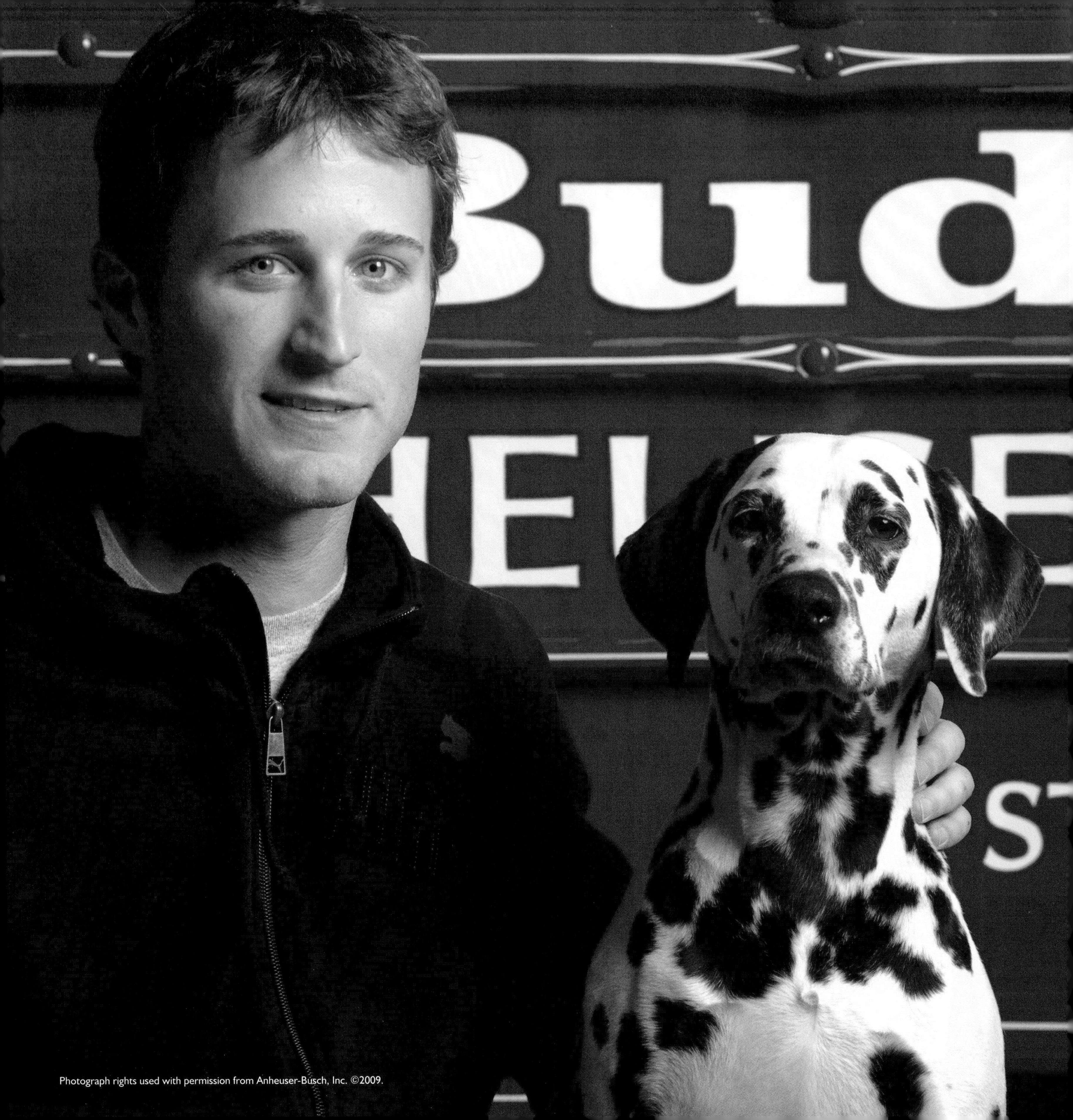
Bud

Kasey Kahne
Doc

"**H**onestly, I've always been a little bit edgy with animals. I grew up on a small farm, and I was always around animals. We had dogs, horses, cows, pigs, and chickens. We even had rabbits for awhile; just a little bit of everything.

"I like animals but am just a little nervous around them because I've had some bad experiences. I've been kicked by them and launched off of them. So it just makes me nervous.

"My best memory was our first dog. His name was Hooker. He was a Doberman Pinscher, and he was the best dog ever to grow up with.

"I know a lot of people would think that Dobermans can be a little bit on the mean side. People would get scared or nervous of him, but to my sister, brother, and me he was our best friend.

"Hooker's the only animal that ever treated me well at the end of the day.

"I had a pony, too. My grandma and grandpa got him for me when I was young. For some reason, he didn't ever want anyone on his back. Every time I would get on him, he would run, turn really fast to get rid of me, or else he would take me to the first tree and clean me off the top of him. So I just quit riding horses.

"It's funny that my sister and brother never had the same problems that I had with animals. They both love animals.

"My sister Shannon actually rescued a boxer named Kalvin, and he is a cool dog. He's kind of like our entire family's dog. Ever since she got Kalvin, I thought that if I decided to get a dog, I would adopt one because it is a cool thing to do."

About Kasey's dog: Doc is seven years old. He is always happy to meet the general public and always looks forward to mealtime. As a member of one of the Clydesdale Touring Hitches, Doc "worked" six Daytona 500 Events, the 2006 St. Louis Cardinals World Series Victory Parade, and has logged over 500,000 miles traveling across the United States. Doc "retired" from the hitch in 2008 and now spends a lot of his down time at the Clydesdale Stables in St. Louis, teaching the next generation of Dalmatians for the Clydesdale Hitch all the "ins and outs" of the job.

Matt Kenseth
Lars, Charlotte, Miley, and Sulley

"**L**ars has been with us the longest. He's an orange tabby cat. I had wanted a cat, and Matt found Lars at an animal hospital in Statesville, North Carolina. He surprised me with Lars.

"It really wasn't long afterwards that we decided to get Charlotte. We figured we were gone from home so much that Lars would probably appreciate some companionship.

"We got Charlotte from a vet in Denver, N.C. Apparently, some guy found her and brought her in, and the vet told him that they didn't accept cats. He couldn't drop the cats off and he couldn't leave the cats there. The guy said he was going to toss her back into the road where he found her, so the vet's office kept her. We went and adopted her.

"Charlotte was only about six-months old when we got her. She was so little that we could hold her in the palm of our hand.

"Just this past winter, we got two more little Tabby cats – Miley and Sulley. We rescued them from a barn in Wisconsin.

"Matt's sister has horses, and she said there was a litter of cats out in the barn. So we went out there. I had really been wanting a little gray cat, which is what Sulley is.

"Of course, I tried picking Sulley up, but that cat was not having it. Every time I picked Sulley up, she clawed me and jumped out of my arms. There was another cat that caught our eye, too. Miley was kind of off to the side and she had caught a mouse. She was eating the mouse, growling at everybody to stay away.

"That first day we didn't end up taking them.

"Later, Matt actually went back to the barn with the intent of getting Sulley. I had joked with Matt and said 'Tell Sulley we got off on the wrong foot, that she's going to be my cat.' So, Matt went back to the barn, but he couldn't just take one. He felt bad taking just one so that's how we ended up with Miley, too.

"He remembered that Miley was the cat in the corner eating the mouse. She was the hunter – kind of like the feisty one, so that's how we got Sulley and Miley.

"They are so playful. We get more entertainment than you could imagine out of just watching the cats play.

"It's been interesting to watch Lars and Charlotte with the two new cats in the house. I don't think Lars plays with them very much, but he likes to follow them around and watch them. He'll keep his eye on them, so I think that forces him to be a little more active than he normally would be. We think he likes them.

"Charlotte, on the other hand, takes turns having issues with the new cats. For the longest

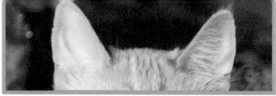

Matt pictured with wife Katie, son Ross, and cats Sulley and Miley

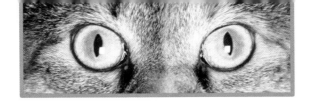

time, she had a big problem with Sulley. She hissed at her every time she came in the room. Now, when Sulley sees Charlotte, Sulley takes two steps back and goes around her. Lately, Charlotte has had a problem with Miley. So, I guess Miley is not giving Charlotte the respect she feels she deserves.

"But we're forcing Charlotte to deal with it. She used to get fed on the counter in the laundry room, but now we feed her on the floor with all the other cats. Whoever she has a problem with that day, we make Charlotte look right at, face to face, and they have to eat face to face. Matt says we brought Charlotte back down to reality. So she's getting a little better.

"Not only have Lars and Charlotte had to get used to the new cats, but the biggest thing for us right now is that we are all getting ready for the baby. I have no idea what to expect. Lars scares me a little bit because he is very territorial.

"Not too long ago though, my niece spent the night with us. The next morning when I was feeding the cats, I couldn't find Miley. It turns out that Miley was beside the bedroom door, just sitting there. It was almost like she was protecting my niece.

"I think Miley will be the nurturing cat, and I would expect the same from Charlotte. Sulley, on the other hand, is a little more hesitant. She gets spooked real easily, so I don't think that Sulley will have a lot to do with the baby for that reason.

"It's going to be interesting for all of us, but I think we'll be just fine."

As told by Katie Kenseth.

Chad Knaus
Shelter Dog AJ

"**I**'ve always been a fan of animals. I love animals. It's just unfortunate that I don't have the time to take care of them. Living in a motor home right now, traveling across the country isn't the right way for me to raise my own personal pet.

"Over the years, I've had a lot of different pets. I've had a German Shepherd, a Chow Chow, a Boxer, a Bengal cat, and even a Monitor lizard.

"When I was younger, I think probably five or six, we had a German Shepherd we named Huggy. We got him as a puppy. Huggy was a big fluff ball. He was a long-haired German Shepherd and was just a beautiful, beautiful dog. We had a good time with him and he was always around when we were working on the race cars. If we went to the lake on an evening off, he would go to the lake with us and swim around. He was awesome.

"Huggy was extremely intimidating to people he didn't know, but for the family environment he was absolutely incredible. He was always very cordial, loving, and protective, and always came up looking for attention. He was a great dog.

"Then several years ago, I had Monty the Lizard. He was cool. He was just a little teeny thing when I got him, and I remember he grew to be about three and a half feet long.

"He was neat. I would let him run around the house. I was pretty poor at the time. All I had was a king-sized bed, but it didn't have a bed frame so it was on the floor. And you know how there are two box springs underneath the king size bed – the two twin size box springs? He would sleep underneath the mattress in between the box springs to keep warm.

"He was a different kind of pet. He would just disappear for weeks on end. You wouldn't see him. He would be hiding in a speaker or under the couch or wherever – there was really no telling. You wouldn't see him for days, and then you would come home and there he would be laying in the sun.

"At the same time I had my Chow Chow Cookie and they didn't get along too well. They would get into barking and hissing matches. It was kind of interesting. They never attacked one another but would cause a lot of commotion.

"Because I've had so many pets, I thought multiple times about getting a dog or even a Bengal cat but I'm just not quite prepared for it right now. Unfortunately, I am gone for days on end and I don't think it's fair for an animal just to sit around.

"Eventually, one day, I'm going to have a few animals and we will see how that all shakes out. I'm looking forward to that day when it actually does happen and I do have a pet at home again." 🐾

About Chad's shelter dog: AJ is a 12-year-old pedigreed German Shepherd who came to Cabarrus Animal Shelter (NC).

Bobby Labonte
Daisy and Chloe

"I've always had some kind of animal. At one point in my life, I had an English Setter, a Poodle and a duck – all at the same time. That's right, I had a duck. It wasn't just a duck, it was a duck that thought it was a dog.

"We had two dog houses in the backyard. There was a big dog house that the two dogs were supposed to share and then the smaller dog house was for the duck. But that's not how it was.

"The duck ruled the backyard. She was actually pretty bossy. So the duck took over the big dog house, and our English Setter and Poodle were having to share the small dog house. The duck even ate their dog food. It was pretty funny.

"One day I came home, and I think our dog had finally had enough. He had grabbed the duck by the neck and was just shaking it. There were duck feathers flying everywhere. I yelled and the dog just dropped the duck and looked at me like 'What? It wasn't me. I didn't do anything.'

"Then, one time we had a crocodile for a couple of weeks. We were really just pet sitting him, I think, but he definitely left an impression on me, especially when I saw him break a plastic fork in half.

"The pets at our house now are a little calmer than what I had as a kid.

"Madison and I rescued Daisy about three years ago. Madison was riding horses at a barn in Thomasville, and there was this dog just hanging out around the barn. She had been somebody's dog, but they had let her out.

"This Lab/Pit Bull mix was just there at the barn, and the guys there started calling her Daisy. I asked them if it was the barn's dog and the answer was no. So then I asked them why they called her Daisy. They said, if no one took her home, she was going to be pushing up the daisies.

"That did it for me right there. Madison and I felt sorry for her, brought her home, and made

Chloe

her part of the family. You've really got to see Daisy to appreciate her. You just have to witness how goofy she is – there's really no way for me to describe it. She is a sweet, sweet, dog and so gentle.

"Then we have Chloe. She's a Chihuahua, and her birthday is on Cinco de Mayo. Chloe sleeps on the back of the couch and falls off while she's sleeping. We all get a laugh out of that.

"Both our dogs are so sweet and they have their own unique personalities. I think it's safe to say that our pets are our family. To me, they're just like my kids. Be good to your animals, and take care of them." 🐾

Left page: Bobby pictured with wife Donna, daughter Madison, son Tyler, and dogs Daisy and Chloe

This page, above: Chloe

Left: Daisy

❝*So then I asked them why they called her Daisy. They said, if no one took her home, she was going to be pushing up the daisies. That did it for me right there. ...[We] brought her home, and made her part of the family.*❞

Claire B. Lang
Rosie

"**T**here is so much in my life that is incredibly stressful. My job is very time oriented. There's not a millisecond to waste. It's fast-paced and go, go, go, all the time.

"In my profession, you have to be perfect. You can't stumble over your words. You have to concentrate and focus. Everything's got to be accurate. You can't flub what you are saying. You always have to be on your mark. You have to be perfect.

"But you don't have to be perfect around a dog. You just be whoever you are. They don't know what your job is. They just love you.

"Rosie – my dog – takes me away from the stress of my job right quick. She slows me down and makes me not think of anything for a while. All she wants is love.

"Rosie is nine years old now. My husband Mike found Rosie when she was six weeks old, and he brought her home in a box. He put the box under this glass-top coffee table that we had.

"He didn't tell me he was going to get a dog. In fact, I had no idea. I walked in and he said, 'I've got a surprise for you.' I walked over to the coffee table, looked down through the glass, and there was the cutest little yellow Lab puppy that you have ever seen.

"Rosie is a great dog. She's a stubborn dog, but she is awesome. She is trained to be a hunting dog. This is a dog that will retrieve over and over and over and you could throw her a stick or anything for days and she would retrieve it for days.

"She is very protective of me and I feel very safe when I have her with me. She's not the kind of dog that will bark incessantly, but she knows what's bad around you. She's not aggressive, but she will let you know if something or somebody is around.

"With our dog Rosie, it doesn't take a lot to make her happy. You just pay her a little attention. I mean come on how much does that require.

"That's why these news stories of animals that have been abused or are not taken care of absolutely tear me up.

"I really believe, if you're going to have an animal, you need to do the right thing with the animal, and you need to care for the animal or don't have one. Let someone else enjoy it because it's really not fair. You see instances of abuse or that sort of thing and a lot of times it's because people don't appreciate what they have, and that just tears me up.

"I just look at Rosie and think about it. It's doesn't take much to make her happy. All she wants is love. All she wants you to do is throw the stick again and again and again. She just loves retrieving it for you.

"She's very sensitive. She's very loving. She's just an awesome dog." 🐾

Steve Letarte
Shelter Dog Lola

"When I'm in the bus lot at the racetrack and somebody is out walking a dog, I usually end up petting and playing with it for a while. I'm a dog lover, and being around dogs is such great therapy. They just love you for you.

"I'm definitely a full-size dog kind of guy. I've always been a fan of both Golden Retrievers and Labs. We don't have a dog right now, but they are the kind of dogs I had growing up.

"We usually had one dog at a time, but we had them for a long, long, time. Misty was a Golden Retriever that I had until I was a teenager. After Misty passed away, we got Sadie, a Black Lab. My parents still have Sadie, and since they live nearby, I get to go play with the dog when I swing by and visit them.

"We don't have any pets now at our house. It wouldn't be fair to the dogs with my schedule because I'm only home three or four days a week for most of the year.

"My little girl Ashlynn is 3, and wants a dog very, very, badly. One of these days we might get one, but we're going to wait until she and her brother Tyler, 5, get a bit older so they can help take care of it.

"We want to wait until they are old enough, not just to help feed and walk the dog, but we want them to be old enough to appreciate the responsibility.

Then we're confident we'll have a dog.

"We think it would be great for them to grow up around dogs. We just want our kids to learn that dogs – pets – are living, breathing, things, that need love and are a responsibility. A dog is a member of the family." 🐾

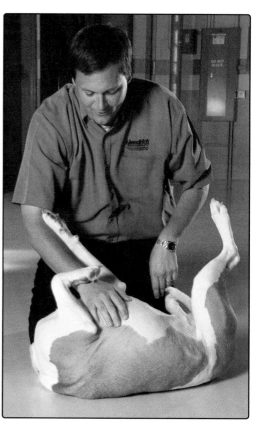

Information on Steve's shelter dog: Lola, a 4-year-old purebred Pit Bull, was rescued by her current owner on the way to the Cabarrus Animal Shelter (NC) where she would likely have been euthanized.

Mark Martin
Shelter Dog Pez

"**I** remember my first dog. His name was Blackie. He was a small black dog, and I found him roaming around the local grocery store parking lot. I don't know what kind of dog he was, but I knew that he was supposed to be my dog. I took him home and named him Blackie.

"Over the years, Arlene and I have had several dogs. We've had a Pomeranian, a Vizsla, and a German Shepherd.

"Jag was the name of our Vizsla, which is a breed of hunting dog. He was the most loving dog. He would play and wrestle with Matt when he was younger. Jag was a very playful dog and he had a very strong body. He was also very smart.

"More recently, we had Uscha who was a German Shepherd. She was a trained protection dog and was particularly fond and protective of Arlene.

About Mark's shelter dog: Pez is an Australian Shepherd. He is a 2-year-old, who was rescued along with 70 other Shepherds from a hoarder. He came to Cascades Humane Society in Jackson, Michigan. He did not know how to act around people or how to play or even how to accept treats when offered to him. With lots of attention and love he opened up to his new world. Pez is now in his new home with lots of room to run and a new doggie playmate.

"To me, pets are the best companions. When you get a dog, he is truly your best friend for life. We have always taken care of our pets like they were one of our children.

"My first dog Blackie was a rescue of sorts. It's a great feeling of comfort that you get from adopting a pet and knowing that you saved that pet's life."

Larry McReynolds
Fontana

"Honestly, I didn't really have my own pet until after Linda and I got married.

"Linda loved Old English Sheep Dogs, so I started searching around for one not long after we got married and found Samantha. We had Samantha for a good 10 years or so.

"When Samantha passed away, I think Linda and I concluded that it was just hard having a dog when you travel as much as we do, but I knew all along that Linda really missed not having a dog. She'd bring it up every once in a while and we'd talk about it but we never pursued it until we got Fontana.

"I can remember distinctly. It was 2001, my first year as a broadcaster with FOX. We did the first half of the season, and then in the second half of the year I did consulting work for Petty Enterprises. We were at Watkins Glen in August of 2001, and I had my headset on. We were either just about to start practice or had just finished practice. I noticed my cell phone kept vibrating. It was Linda.

"I looked at my phone and pulled my headset back and called her. She obviously knew to catch me at a bad moment or the right moment, whichever way you want to look at it. She said 'Larry, I have found a dog at the pet store, and I really love this dog. Larry, he is a trouble free type dog, very easily house broken. They don't shed. I know you're not big on a house dog, but this dog doesn't shed.'

"I said 'Linda, I'm in the middle of practice at Watkins Glen. Whatever you want to do, that's fine.'

"Sure enough, when I got home on Sunday night, this little Peekapoo met me at the door. So obviously, with me semi-giving the green light, Linda went out and bought Fontana.

"Fontana's got a little loveseat couch in our living room that is his territory. He lays on that loveseat I think 20 hours out of the 24 hour day. I'll see him lying over there, and he might raise his head up. I tell people that are visiting that 'that's high gear right there, that's as active as he is going to probably get.'

"But if it is just after dark and one of us gets up and makes a move in the direction of the bedroom, Fontana is off that loveseat and into the bedroom. In his mind, it's time to go to bed and he's the first one in the bed. What's funny is, he sleeps at the end of the bed, but when I'm not home, he'll sleep right there on my side.

"He's got some phobias, too. He hates fireworks and hot air balloons. He is absolutely petrified of jack-o-lanterns that we put outside for Halloween.

"When we put the satellite dish in at the house a few years ago, they put it in his territory where he goes to the bathroom. It was several weeks before that dog would even go near that area, to the point that I even called the Direct TV guy, and asked if the dish put out some kind of sound wave that humans couldn't hear but dogs could hear thinking, maybe that's why Fontana wouldn't go over there. He told me no.

"Maybe it's not a good correlation, but I've always said that dogs and cats in some small way are like babies. Animals don't ask to come into this world. It's totally God's will that any pet is born.

"I just think it's the obligation of human beings to care for these animals, to take care of them, and to give them love. I guess my encouragement is that if you're going to make a commitment to get a dog or a cat, you've got to make the commitment to take care of it as well.

"It can't just be a toy you play with once a day. You've got to let him go to the bathroom. You've got to feed him. You've got to water him. You've got to make sure he gets to the vet to get all his proper shots and care. That's the obligation we have – to take care of our pets."

Larry with wife Linda, daughter Kendall, and dog Fontana

“I just think it's the obligation of human beings to care for these animals, to take care of them, and to give them love. I guess my encouragement is that if you're going to make a commitment to get a dog or a cat, you've got to make the commitment to take care of it as well.”

Casey Mears
Nash

"**T**he thing I like about Nash is that he is a small dog, but he is a small dog who thinks he is a big dog.

"Trish had Nash before we got together. He's a Yorkshire Terrier, but he's not like any lap dog I've ever been around. Nash kind of has a big dog mentality and that's fun for me because I've always liked bigger dogs.

"He really likes being outside. He likes playing fetch with balls. He even jumps in the pool. We'll throw a ball in the pool and he'll jump into the pool after it. It's funny to see this little dog do things like that.

"We'll have him around somewhere, and people will say how much they love him and that they want to know what kind of dog he is because they would like to have one like him. I always tell them that I don't think he is a very good representative of a Yorkie.

"Nash had always been Trish's baby, so when Samantha, our daughter, came into the picture last November, he had a hard time figuring her out.

"He's still skeptical about her because she is so young, but Sam just absolutely loves Nash. We'll give her the ball sometimes and she'll wave it around and he will start barking at her. She just loves it. She laughs and laughs. Anytime he walks by in front of her, she laughs. She just loves watching him.

"I think as Sam gets a little bit older, we'll get a puppy that she can kind of grow up with. I always had pets and animals growing up. At one point in time we had chickens, pigs, and goats. I've had a beagle, I've had a Lab. I had a couple of mutts, cats, turtles, lizards, and snakes. I had ferrets. I even had a rat at one point.

I remember as a kid just loving having a dog. They love you regardless. They are always happy to see you. I always looked forward to seeing my dog when I came home. I think that's what it is more than anything.

"I want Sam to have the same experience with animals as she grows up. We have some ideas about what kinds of pets we are wanting. I know that Trish would really like to get her a rabbit. The new house we are living in has a pond and there are turtles in it, so that will be fun for her. I'm sure Sam will be close to plenty of animals.

"I remember as a kid how much I loved having a dog. They love you regardless. They are always happy to see you. I always looked forward to seeing my dog when I came home. I think that's what it is more than anything.

"You don't really teach your child about pets. I mean, obviously, you teach them to pet them gently and not to be rough with them, but I think, more than anything, they just learn what pets mean to them on their own.

"I want Sam to have that experience with animals, and I want her to have that type of companionship."

Casey pictured with wife Trish, daughter Sam, and dog Nash

Ryan Newman
Digger, Harley, Mopar, Socks, Fred, and Dunkin

"**O**ur family has grown in the past few years. On Thanksgiving Day 2007, I was driving around our farm property and came across two stray dogs. When I stopped my truck, they came right up to me. They were full of dirt, fleas and ticks, so I decided to bring them home, clean them up and look for their owners. Krissie and I had just moved into our new home and had family coming over for dinner. We put the dogs into our pen and waited for our guests to leave before we went out and cleaned them up.

"Both dogs were very well mannered and seemed to get along with the rest of our pack. Krissie put signs up in the neighborhood, notified the papers and local animal groups, but no one claimed the two. We named them Piglet and Fred. I grew attached to Fred quickly. He would go everywhere with me. Until one day they escaped from our fence and went out for a stroll. A neighbor had caught Fred and called us that night; it was a few days later before Piglet came strolling back into the yard.

"A week or so later, Piglet decided to go out again. Krissie spent the whole day searching our neighborhood for her. Then a gentleman called her and said Piglet was in his front yard. Krissie went over to pick Piglet up and she was sitting on the gentleman's front porch. No one was home, so Krissie put Piglet in her truck and headed home. Another week goes by and Piglet gets out again. Krissie searches for her all day and finally heads down to where she picked Piglet up the last time. Sure enough, Piglet was out in that guy's front yard! Krissie knocked on the door and the gentleman came out. He said he was just about to call her and notify her that Piglet was back. Krissie apologized for bothering him and said she was not sure why Piglet kept coming back to his yard.

He then explained to her that she used to be his dog and he figured she had run off, been hit by a car or picked up by Animal Control. Krissie was floored and did not want the guy to think she was stealing his dog. I mean why would he not tell her that the first time he called her to pick Piglet up! Krissie said he was welcome to have his dog back and that they had been living with us for months. The gentleman then notified her that Fred was his dog as well. He did not want either dog back and said they looked like they were happy and being well cared for. He had

Mopar, Fred and Dunkin

several other dogs and did not miss Fred and Piglet (originally named Paco and Daisy). So Piglet came back home with Krissie.

"Our oldest dog, Digger is our pack leader. When Piglet came back home, she and Digger were not getting along so well. We tried sending the two of them to Boot Camp training, so they could learn how to get along, but sometimes two dogs are just not meant to be in the same pack. We had some of our good friends in town from California visiting. They fell in love with Piglet and asked us if they could take her home. Knowing that she and Digger were constantly fighting, it was the best thing we could do for both dogs. Piglet is now living in sunny California with our good friends and her best dog friend Duke. We get to visit her every time we go out racing in California. Fred is still with us and became number 5 in our pack.

"I thought we were done adding dogs, until April 2009 when Krissie dropped me off at the airport to go to Talladega. When I landed there was a message on my phone that she had rescued another dog and was on her way to our vet's office with him."

As told by Ryan Newman

"When I dropped Ryan off at the airport, I decided to go through my usual routine of stopping at Dunkin' Donuts for coffee. When I came around the drive through, below the pick up window was a dog. I asked the employees how long he had been there and they told me he came and went for about a month. They said people had tried to catch him but no one was able to get close enough. Of course I couldn't just drive away. I pulled over into a parking space, and called my uncle to bring me a leash and collar. The employees from Dunkin' Donuts were nice enough to give me some sausage to lure the dog close enough to catch him. My uncle and I chased this dog around the Dunkin' Donuts parking lot for two and a half hours. We would get close enough to pet him, but as soon as I tried to slip the collar on, he would take off. I did not want to chase him toward the busy street. The only thing left I could think of doing was to call Animal Control out to help trap him. Animal Control was out there within minutes and brought me a trap. After several unsuccessful attempts and getting him in the trap, we finally caught him with a leash and a can of cat food.

"After he was on the leash he just sat there like the game was over. Because he was so calm and did not show any signs of aggression, Animal Control let me take him with me.

"The only appropriate name for him was Dunkin' Donuts. We took him to our vet, and brought him home to see how he would do with our pack. He was so submissive and just wanted to love on everyone. I tried finding his owner, yet no one claimed him. I was so attached to his sweet demeanor, I couldn't help but keeping him. We changed his name after he came back from being fixed. His new name is now Dunkin No Nuts! He is the perfect addition to our family, even though he has a few bad stray habits we need to work on.

"Our pack is pretty balanced now, we have three males and three females. We love spending time with our kids, and we miss them when we are traveling to all of the races. I could not imagine our lives without them, they bring so much happiness and laughter into our home. Take care of your pets, and they will take care of you."

As told by Krissie Newman 🐾

Ryan pictured with wife Krissie, and dogs Mopar, Harley, Fred, Digger, Dunkin and Socks

Right: Krissie pictured with dog Mopar

"Take care of your pets, and they will take care of you."

Max Papis
Batu, Zoe, and Mya

"**W**hen I was very pregnant with our first son Marco, I borrowed somebody's camera and took pictures of all the animals, who I call Marco's brothers and sisters. So, in his room there are pictures of the pets because they are his family. I think that we are all a family, whether you're a cat, a dog, or a kid, we are all equal in this family.

"We have lots of dogs and cats. The three dogs are Batu, Zoe, and Mya and the four cats are Bono, Nini, Twiggy, and Stinky.

"Batu was our first child. We call her our angel child because she is the most well behaved. She's very scared of lightning and thunder. One night she was trembling. I think I was really tired and I made Batu leave because she was lying on top of my legs. A little later I woke up, and she was in our son's crib next to us, sleeping with him, because she was so scared of the thunder and lightning. I thought it was very cute that she found comfort in this little baby.

"I really wanted to get another dog to get Batu company, and that's how we got Zoe. I went to a few humane societies in Miami to look for a dog. I found Zoe, and she was the last one of a litter of seven. She had the saddest look on her face, and she just broke my heart, so that was it.

"I didn't tell Max I was going to get another dog. So for two days, every time Max would call, I would go to the closet and answer the phone just so Max wouldn't hear her bark. I went to the airport to pick Max up and he opened the back door of the car and tiny Zoe was just barking at him. She was this little, itty, bitty thing and I said, "This is your new daughter."

"Zoe is very pretty. She's the biggest of our three dogs. She's about the size of a small Lab.

"We got Mya here in Iredell County at the animal shelter. I actually went there to get something for one of my dogs. I was leaving and got drawn into the room with puppies and dogs. I was very pregnant with my second son Mateo, and thought it would be really cool for my older son Marco to have his own dog since this baby was coming.

"So we got Mya. She looks and acts like a beagle. She chews up everything. We just redid our irrigation system, and she has chewed it up three times. We have to put up child gates everywhere so that she can't

Left: Max pictured with dogs Batu, Zoe, and Mya

Right: Max pictured with wife Tati, sons Marco and Mateo, and dogs, Batu, Zoe, and Mya

have access to some areas of the house when we're not home because she's really bad.

"I was an assistant tech at a vet in Miami. I had just graduated, majoring in psychology, advertising, and marketing. I was already traveling with Max to the races. One day, when I was there with my pets, they asked me – if I would be interested in helping out.

"They said they would work with my schedule because they knew that I traveled. So I said "okay." I worked there for about a year until I got pregnant. That's how we ended up with Nini, Bono, and Twiggy.

"Stinky was a very mean cat in a neighborhood in Miami, and we managed to tame him. Stinky is a real Tom cat. He has half an ear and half a tail. We really rescued him the night of Hurricane Katrina. We had fed him for two weeks at home after we had found him almost dead underneath our car. The night of Hurricane Katrina, he just let me pick him up and put him in a room and I managed to tame him that night. He's been home since then. But he's sick. He has FIV (feline immunodeficiency virus) He's not going to be with us too long.

"For sure, having all our rescued animals brings a lot of craziness, but that's what we like. We're the family that when somebody finds a dog or a cat, they will call us to see if we can foster them or keep them. It brings so much joy.

"I don't think our life would be complete without animals. It's hard, and it gets very expensive with all the runs to the vet because you need to take care of your pets like you take care of your kids. I think it takes a lot of responsibility even if you have just one. It is as difficult as having the seven that we have. It's the same responsibility – if you have it with one, you have it with the rest. You need to take a lot of responsibility and be aware that taking care of an animal is like taking care of a child. They require that much attention, too.

"I think, especially now that we have kids, the relationship of kids with pets is so important for their growth and for their health. I wouldn't have it any other way. This is who the Papis family is."
As told by Tatiana Papis

Robin Pemberton
Chaos, Ariel, Penny, Loafer, Chris Heron, Kessy, Boomer, and Mac

"I think I was meant to have 10 children. I don't know. Anytime I am some place, and I see an animal, I want to bring them home. I wouldn't change it though. I love them. They are my companions.

"My kids, Bray and Briggs, are grown and gone now. My husband, Robin, is gone all the time. And so, they're my company. I am surrounded by my big family. They follow me up the stairs. They follow me into the bathroom. They follow me downstairs.

"You always have a group of animals with you. It does make for an eventful environment. We have seven dogs.

"Chaos is a miniature Doberman Pinscher. He's the oldest of the bunch, about 10. He loves to go to the lake and dig, and dig, and dig.

"Ariel is a German Shepherd/Collie mix. She's kind of the matriarch of the family. She's a little bit of a loner. She stays on the front porch and guards everything. She was an adoptee from the Rock Hill Humane Society. When I first got her, they thought she had distemper and would not live. She's nine now and she's done all kinds of stuff.

"Penny is a long-haired Dachshund, and she is in love with Robin. She is his girl. She won't get out of bed unless he is up. She won't leave the front of the shower while he is in there. She just shadows him.

"And then we have Loafer, who is a short-haired Dachshund. She thinks she is a big dog and it gets her into trouble. Sometimes she pays the consequences for that. She's had to have surgery because she has gotten into a tussle with the big dogs before.

"My son found Chris Heron on Highway 21 and brought him home. He is a Chow/Retriever mix, and he is a lug. Chris Heron was a black-balled basketball player, and our oldest son played basketball, so that's where he got his name. Chris Heron is a really laid-back dog, and he has a really funny personality. He hangs with the kids. He gets taken to eat cheeseburgers. He wears his Panthers uniform. He drinks beer. He is a funny dog.

"Kessy is a black German Shepherd. She came from a lineage of Schutzhund level three-trained dogs. She is quite an intense dog. I was going to train her as a protection dog, but just could not keep her separate from the other dogs.

"Mac is also a black German Shepherd, and he's a really laid-back dog. He is in the process right now of getting double hip-replacement. He has severe dysplasia. He just had knee surgery

and he goes back to NC State for a follow-up appointment. His hips and knees are so bad, they were thinking of amputating his leg, but we're going to try to see if there is something that can be done to give his knee enough stability so that they can do the hip replacement surgery.

"We both love them so much. Robin loves them. There have been times he has not been pleased because I'm bringing home another dog, but once they enter the door, they are ours.

"Penny was really for my mother but she couldn't keep her, so I brought her home and went to work to find a place for her. When I came home and told Robin that I had somebody that would take Penny, he said, 'You go tell them to find their own Dachshund.' He wouldn't give her up.

"Once they make it through the door, they are here. It's really like having kids. You've got a myriad of personalities. Some get along better than others. Some have health issues. Most of them are fairly healthy. Right now we are battling a little hip dysplasia with one of our dogs and some domination problems once in a while. But that's few and far between. Most of the time, everyone is fairly good."

As told by Lisa Pemberton

"I love them. They are my companions."

Robin pictured with wife Lisa, sons Bray and Briggs, and dogs Ariel, Chaos, Penny, Loafer, Chris Heron, Kessy, Mac, and Boomer

Kyle Petty
Miah, Lulu, Mattie, Jojo, Hawk, and Spurs

VICTORY JUNCTION GANG
Founded for kids in honor of Adam Petty

Kyle pictured with wife Pattie, dogs Miah, LuLu, Mattie, and Spurs, pony Jojo, and horse Hawk

"**P**ets have always been a big part of our lives. We love animals, and we love having them as part of our home.

"Over the years, we have had a lot of pets. Back when I raced out of a shop in Charlotte, one of the guys on the team rescued this dog named, Digger. He didn't have a place to keep her at the time. So we brought her back to the farm where she lived a very happy life with all our other animals – horses, dogs, you name it.

"In our family for some reason, we love to give animals to each other. The kids and I have given Pattie dogs over the years. And the two mini-Australian Shepherds that we have at the Victory Junction Gang Camp now – Mattie and Spurs – were gifts to Montgomery Lee as congratulations on doing well in her horse competitions.

"LuLu and Tonka are our Pomeranians.

"Tonka is the newest addition to our family. I got Tonka for Pattie just a few months ago because her other dog, Miah, was sick. Pattie really loves her little dogs, and I have to admit that so do I. When Miah got sick, it was really hard on Pattie, so I decided to get her another little dog just in case something happened.

"Unfortunately Miah, who had been given to Pattie by Montgomery Lee, passed away. Our daughter had given Pattie the pup when she moved away to school. Montgomery Lee thought the small, orange dog would help her mom with her 'empty nest' syndrome. She was a huge part of our family, and we miss her so much.

"Because we have always had animals, I think it's only natural that we work to share our love of animals with the kids at Victory Junction Gang Camp. At the camp, we have about 12 horses, four mini-ponies, five mini-donkeys, two llamas, and goats. We also have cows and pigs that come and 'visit' during the summer camp sessions, and we are always looking for new animals.

"We have donated several of our animals to the camp. Chip was my son Austin's horse, and we knew he would be the perfect horse for the kids because he is so gentle and smart. He is probably the best camp horse we have, and if you ask the kids, I think he is the No. 1 favorite horse at camp.

"Hawk and Ricki are horses we have donated, too. We work really hard to try to recruit animals and have animals donated to our camp, so the children can enjoy them.

"Most of what we do these days revolves around working with the animals at our camp and recruiting animals to be donated to our program here. I strongly believe in what we are doing here with animals and what Humane Societies are doing, too. I encourage people to participate in volunteering as well as adoption or rescue. Our animals have been a very special and important part of our lives." 🐾

Richard Petty
Queenie

"**I** grew up around animals because I lived out in the country. So, I just kind of expected all my kids and grandkids to grow up around animals too, just so they would have some respect for other forms of life besides human life.

"I always had a dog growing up, mostly, German Shepherds. After Kyle was born, he had a Newfoundland. It was a big black dog and we named him Hemi, like a Hemi engine in my Dodge. I really think we have had just about everything at some point in time except a bulldog.

"Now, we've got Corgis, buffalo, long horns, horses, miniature donkeys, miniature goats, goats, turkeys, chickens, ducks, guineas, peacocks, and I'm sure I'm missing something.

"I just decided one day I wanted a buffalo, so I ended up getting a couple of them.

"We've got about a dozen guineas. Some folks right up the road here had some, so we got a pair of guineas and raised them. Now we have 12. They are the messiest things you have ever seen, and they do a lot of squealing and squawking.

"We've got about six peacocks about a quarter-mile back in the woods. We started with a pair, and now they're sitting on some eggs again, so we'll have more.

"Of course, we've got all the animals that are just around our house because of where we live. We can sit on the back porch and watch the deer run across the back yard. We watch fox, opossums,

Richard with his buffalo

I think there's just something about animals – it doesn't matter if you're a kid or an adult – just being around animals soothes you. I think that's the reason why people like dogs so much. It brings them back to earth and soothes them.

Linda pictured with dog Queenie

and 'coons run across. We've got a little bit of everything because we live way out in the country.

"I think there's just something about animals – it doesn't matter if you're a kid or an adult – just being around animals soothes you. I think that's the reason why people like dogs so much. It brings them back to earth and soothes them.

"That's why having the animals at Victory Junction Gang Camp has been such a good thing. When the kids read about animals or see them on TV, that's one thing – they can say they've seen animals. When they come to camp, they can actually go in and pet them all or ride the horse around, or just see the animals up close. It's a real riot for them.

"I think they really, really get a lot out of it. And so do we." 🐾

David Reutimann
Shotzy, Daisy, and Roxy

"The original pony that started this whole thing for us was Shotzy.

"Michael's (Waltrip) daughter Macy was riding horses, and Emilia thought she might like to take some lessons. The lady who was giving Macy some lessons had Shotzy the Pony. She actually had a lot of horses, and she was trying to cut back a little bit.

"Emilia, who is seven now, had started riding Shotzy and taking lessons on him, and she kind of fell in love with him. So that ended up being Emilia's Christmas present in 2007. And that's kind of how it started.

"We did some things with Michael and ended up getting this place and building the barn in 2008. It's nice and quiet out here.

"Once we got the barn, we got Teddy, an Appaloosa and Lisa's horse. Lisa always wanted horses because her grandfather had them.

"Then we got the donkeys – Angelina and Shania. Only one of those donkeys is quote unquote "mine." Shania is actually Shane Wilson's. Shane wanted a donkey and I think I ended up being donkey-owner by default because they came as a package deal, and he needed a place to keep his.

"Mine for some reason – Angelina – doesn't really like me. Emilia tells me it's because I don't spend enough time with her. She says that I need to come out here every day and bring her treats every time. She may be on to something.

"We also have two barn cats, Tigger and Callie, who kind of just migrated over to our barn and took up residence.

"At home, we have our two Dachshunds, Daisy and Roxy. Daisy is actually the first pet that Lisa and I got, she's about 10 years old now. Roxy came along a few years ago. They're great dogs and they can come out here with us and travel with us.

"They're small and they're easy to take care of. You have to make sure they don't jump off of things and act crazy like that. For the most part, they are pretty low-maintenance dogs. They are very, very, affectionate and we have a lot of fun with them.

"Being out here is relaxing. I was never a horse person at all, and I'm still not entirely sure that I am, but they are great animals. They have attitudes, good days, and bad, and mannerisms just like people do.

"It's pretty amazing, watching them running around – how much power they have and how awesome they are. They are neat animals. So I've enjoyed that aspect of it. They are a lot of work, as most things are. But for now, this is what Emilia likes to do. As long as she enjoys it, we'll keep doing it.

"For me, the most important thing is that Emilia really enjoys the horses and she seems to

have a good time spending time with the animals and doing the things that she does with them.

"In the end, I have to travel a lot. Emilia needs to have what she wants to do and things that are important to her.

"That's why we do what we do – so Emilia can learn. It teaches her responsibility. It teaches her patience. She has to clean the stalls and brush the horses. She has to pick their hooves and lead the horses around the field. She has to take care of them.

"She doesn't necessarily care for the patience and responsibility part, but it makes her understand that, in order for you to have things that you like, there's work involved in all that. That's a valuable lesson that I can't think of any better way for her to learn than through having pets." 🐾

David pictured with wife Lisa, and daughter Emilia on pony Shotzy

It teaches her responsibility. It teaches her patience. She has to clean the stalls and brush the horses. She has to pick their hooves and lead the horses around the field. She has to take care of them. She doesn't necessarily care for the patience and responsibility part, but it makes her understand that in order for you to have things that you like, there's work involved in all that. That's a valuable lesson that I can't think of any better way for her to learn than through having pets.

Doug Richert
Pee Wee, May, Daisy, Pedo, Rusty, Indy, Mini, Miss Pitty, Rowdy, Springer, Tensile, and Harley

"**O**ne person can't save all the animals out there that need homes, but one person can make a difference. That's always been our philosophy when it comes to animals, and we have done everything in our power to help as many animals as we can over the years.

"Our desire to rescue and help these animals started way back when. In fact, our very first dog together was saved from an abusive home in Charlotte. His name was Oscar and he was a black poodle.

"I was working with Junior Johnson at that time, and down the road from the race shop was a gas station. Robin was there getting gas one day not long after we had rescued Oscar, and while she was there she found Friskie. So we went from having no pets, to two in no time.

"That's kind of how it all got started. We loved pets, and rescuing unwanted animals seemed to be the perfect way for us to make a difference. All our pets are spayed and neutered because we don't want to add to an already bad problem of pet overpopulation. We wish that there was a law making spaying and neutering affordable and a must for all pet owners. But until that time, we will just encourage others to do what is best for the animals.

"All of our pets have come from shelters, the side of road, or even from owners who would just leave their dogs tied up in the yard day in and day out. We would see a dog tied up in the yard and see that no one was paying attention to it, so we would go and ask the owner about it. Every time without fail, the owner told us they didn't want the pet, so we will bring the dog home with us.

"Right now, we have 12 dogs and seven cats. That's a house full, but that's our family.

"Pee Wee is about eight-years-old and is a four-and-a-half pound black poodle mix. He was brought into a local vet after he was found wandering the streets. The vet called us, and we couldn't say no.

"Three of our dogs are pugs – May, Daisy and Pedo. They are brothers and sisters. We had rescued their mother, and she died while giving birth to them. Robin was the 'momma dog' for the puppies, feeding them every two hours for the first five weeks of their lives. They traveled all over the country with us before they even opened their eyes. They're nearly five-years-old now, and they are by far the most loving dogs.

"Five of our dogs came from a shelter – Rusty, Indy, Mini, Miss Pitty, and Rowdy. They

> **We see ourselves as a voice for the animals that don't have a voice. We treasure having each and every animal in our life. They are a blessing.**

all had sores and scars. They were scared and very timid. Now, they are very healthy and loving.

"Our other three dogs were just given up by their owners. Springer was left on the door step of a friend's house. He had a toy and some food with him and the note that was tied to him said 'Here's a dog for you.' Springer gets his name honestly – he jumps like a bug.

"Both Tensile's and Harley's owners just didn't want them, so we ended up adding them to our brood. Tensile is a very obedient dog. Harley is still a puppy, and he is growing like a weed. Harley's a big mutt, and you just want to love him.

"Just like the dogs, all seven of the cats have been rescued by us. Nash probably has the best story. Nash was found in a team hauler at Nashville Superspeedway when I was working in the truck series with Carl Edwards.

"Nash was about four weeks old then, and it was another one of our animals that Robin bottle fed and babied to keep healthy. The cool thing about Nash is that he went to Victory Lane with us the night we found him.

"Having one pet is a big responsibility, let alone the group that we have. But it is a responsibility that we love and we wouldn't trade.

"I wish that everyone would just go to the pound once, look at all the animals there, and see all those sad eyes looking at them. It's a sight that will never be erased from anyone's mind, and I think that people might treat animals differently if they did that.

"For us, we just want to do all that we can to help the animals. We donate to groups like Pug Rescue of North Carolina and the Canine Seizure Assist Group. When we hear about others that need help, we do what we can.

"We see ourselves as a voice for the animals that don't have a voice. We treasure having each and every animal in our life. They are a blessing."

Doug pictured with wife Robin and dogs Pee Wee, May, Daisy, Pedo, Rusty, Indy, Mini, Miss Pitty, Rowdy, Springer, Tensile, and Harley

Morgan Shepherd
Charger and Bella

"I've got a lot of animal stories. I've had all kinds of animals.

"Over the years, I've raised a little bit of everything, whether it's squirrels, flying squirrels, raccoons, goats, or whatever. As a matter of fact, raising flying squirrels was how I bought my first car. When I was 12, I traded two flying squirrels, a gray squirrel and a 20-gauge shot gun plus $12.50 for my first car – a 1937 Chevy.

"Raccoons are really neat animals. They are real family oriented. I had this one raccoon named Citgo. I had him back when I was with the Wood Brothers and that was our sponsor. He was a blonde raccoon, and we raised him and our German Shepherd together – his name was Shep.

"They were quite a treat to the family. I took Citgo to Daytona with us. I took him a lot of places. He would go over to the store, and everybody would feed him when he came in. He was just a good old boy. He would go swimming with the kids in the pool and just swim up to everybody. There wasn't a mean bone in his body. A lot of raccoons get real mean, but he was unusual.

"I always joked that Citgo was really good with my lawyer. My lawyer came over one day and sat on the sofa. My raccoon went over to my lawyer, stuck his hand in his pocket, and pulled his money out and brought it to me. He was quite a treat.

"Citgo was with us about 14 years before we had an accident and he died.

"Now, we have Charger, a German Shepherd and Bella, a Pomeranian. We named Charger back when we were with Dodge. Charger is three years old, and he is about more than we can handle. He's pretty rambunctious, and it's hard to keep him still, but he is a good dog. He just loves to be loved.

"Believe it or not, Charger was actually one of these 'freebie' dogs. I was doing an appearance down at Myrtle Beach and this guy came up and he had this beautiful German Shepherd. We had just put my dog Shep down because of some health issues, and I told the man that I would like to find another German Shepherd.

"He said, 'Believe it or not, my female is pregnant right now. I won't sell you one, but I will give you one.' He gave us Charger.

"I laugh because Charger didn't cost us anything until we got him home. I sent him to school for about six weeks, and spent like $950 on him for training. As soon as I got him out of school, he took off and went all over the neighborhood. We couldn't find him that night.

"We found him the next morning and unfortunately a car had hit him. We went to the vet and he was all broken up. The lady there

Morgan pictured with wife Cindy and dogs Charger and Bella

asked us what we wanted to do. I told her I couldn't lose my friend, to just fix him. So he's got steel pins in his hip. You can't tell it though. He healed really well.

"When it was all said and done, I think we ended up having about $4,000 in this 'free' dog. But he's a good dog, and he's getting calmer as he gets a little bit of age on him.

"Bella goes with us to the races. She's a little bigger Pomeranian than what our other ones were in the past, but she's been a blessing to us. She is quite entertaining. She'll get her toys and throw them up in the air and play with them. She'll play all by herself. Cindy feeds her and takes care of her, but she's a daddy's girl.

"My animals have really been a treat for me over the years." 🐾

❝We went to the vet and he was all broken up. The lady there asked us what we wanted to do. I told her I couldn't lose my friend, to just fix him.❞

Mike Skinner
Tundra

❝Opus was our first dog, and that's really where the story starts. Everybody knew Opus.

"Opus had some issues, and passed away. Soon after he passed, one of the charities that we give to in Florida gave Angie a call. It was the Animal Rescue and they had a little Dobie puppy who was the only survivor in his litter. They asked if we would consider rescuing him. We went to look at him and of course it was love at first sight for Angie. That's how Tundra came along.

"We also have two cats. After we built our dream house in Florida about five years ago, we heard a noise up in the house. It was the middle of July in Florida, and it was hotter than heck but I climbed up in the attic.

"I could see that there were three little kittens in there, but I couldn't get to them. We had to have the carpenters come out, cut the soffit out of the house and rescue these little kitties.

"We ended up keeping two of them – Soffit, because that's where the kittens were and Angie wanted to name the other one Mike because he was mean as could be, but we ended up calling him Spike instead. We adopted the third one, Spruce, out. They've been with us ever since.

"Neither one of us were really cat people, but they just kind of came with the house. We rescued them and had to bottle feed them. The cats and Tundra were both our babies. We got them way early and it was before they should have been away from their mothers, but they were abandoned. We just had to be the mom to all of them.

"All our animals were rescued, and we try to do a lot to help out charities that take care of animals, children, and the elderly.

"We have a golf outing and then a hoe-down bash with live music and food. It is a blast. It's called the Toyota Tundra Skinner Round-Up. It's a great event and we just really have a lot of fun with it. And while we are having fun, we're able to give money to these local charities and help people."

As told by Mike Skinner

"Actually, the whole reason we started the Skinner Round-up for Charity was because of Animal Rescue and Animal Charity. I was working on various events with different people just trying to help raise money in the community because I feel like Mike and I have been blessed to live this great lifestyle and we wanted to give back.

"I was considering doing our own charity event, but I wasn't sure about it. So one day, I was in the hair salon and this lady walked in. She had two puppies that she just found on the side of the road, and it just so happened that she had an animal rescue called Second Chance. I

just started talking to her, asking her how much money she needed to operate for a year and things like that. That was my sign.

"We did our first tournament that year and made $125,000. That was just basically a golf event and a little casino night party at a country club. It's now turned into a really big event.

"We work a lot with Concerned Citizens for Animal Welfare. They raise money so people can get their animals spayed and neutered. In my opinion, that's the biggest problem. That's how we end up with an overflow of animals that don't have homes and animals that don't have a choice.

"It's not really fair for the animals. People need to get their pet spayed or neutered. In the end, that's better for the pet.

"I want to do more for the animals because our animals have been such an important part of our lives. We just bought a new house with 16 acres. I want to build a barn for rescue dogs. I want to get dogs and try to find a home for them.

"I actually helped Lynne and AJ Allmendinger pick out their dog, Misty. I told them when they were looking for a dog, that getting a dog was the best thing they would ever do.

"When we are at the racetrack, Tundra is truly our best buddy. For the wives, I think it's great to have an animal because it gives us something to do and someone to spend time with at the track. When racing is over for the day, the husbands can come in and there are the dogs. No matter if they were the last car or the fastest car, dogs don't know, they still want to play ball.

"We've been very lucky that our race team all enjoys Tundra. They always come to our motor coach after the garage closes, and they always play with him. Tundra is the love of our race team.

"We started coming up to North Carolina because we lived in Florida, and we would park our bus right next to the race shop. So Tundra became the shop dog. Recently, the guys were doing pit practice and apparently he was chasing our tire changers around the car, nipping at their butts.

"At the Texas race, our pit crew was over the top amazing. They were all laughing and joking that it was because they were scared to death that Tundra was going to bite them if they didn't go fast enough. So, he's the new pit stop coach.

"Tundra is just in love with this race team because they are so playful."

As told by Angie Skinner

> *"All our animals were rescued, and we try to do a lot to help out charities that take care of animals, children, and the elderly."*

Mike pictured with wife Angie and dog Tundra

Regan Smith
Champ, Princess, Lamar, Belle, and Magoo

"With our whole family being involved in rescuing and trying to adopt animals out, I've seen how many people get really good animals that didn't have homes before they adopted them.

"My mom (Lee) has spearheaded our overall family involvement in working with animals. We have always cared a lot about animals, and animals have always been a really big part in all our lives.

"I couldn't tell you how many dogs I have had since I was a kid.

"We've always had Doberman Pinschers. We had a couple of other little dogs and cats, too, but I remember us mostly having Dobermans.

"They get a bad rap sometimes and they are the most loyal, faithful dogs you will ever meet. They are just great animals when they are raised right. They are really cool to have around and they will stand by you and protect you.

"Right now we have three Dobermans and two dogs that are both under five pounds that run around the same house and play and live together. It's cool. It gives us something to keep us busy, as if we're not busy enough with racing already.

"Champ, Lamar, and Belle are our Dobermans. I've had Champ since I was 18 and he's my boy.

"Lamar was a rescue dog that we got from Atlanta. He was abused in his original home, and the abuse was so bad that the vet actually had to amputate his paw.

"We were a little concerned with him only having three legs as to how well he would get along with Champ, but he holds his own. Not only is he faster than Champ, I think he is meaner when they fight, too. He's really just a big baby. He would rather be in people's laps all the time.

"We got Belle as a rescue from New York. She's a red Doberman, and she's about as perfect look-wise as a dog could get. She is so young. She just loves to play, and run, and just go nuts.

"Princess was a Christmas present for my girlfriend Megan, and Magoo is from the Iredell Humane Society.

"With most of our pets coming from rescues, I know there are really good animals that need homes. As crazy as it sounds, it seems like an adoptive dog is actually more appreciative when they get in a good home. They are really good pets when they finally get to a good home.

"We have had at least 10 to 15 rescue animals in the past year that have been at the office or stayed with us for an extended period of time and it's tough to get rid of them because they are really cool animals. There are just so many good animals out there that don't have homes. Why people don't spay and neuter their pets is beyond me. It's simple and, in a lot of cases, there are organizations that basically pay for this service.

"So, we just keep trying to get the word out to people about adoption and being responsible with their pets. There are too many animals without homes." 🐾

Top left to right:
Princess, Mr. Magoo

Bottom left to right:
Bella, Lamar and Champ

With most of our pets coming from rescues, I know there are really good animals that need homes. As crazy as it sounds, it seems like an adoptive dog is actually more appreciative when they get in a good home. They are really good pets when they finally get to a good home.

Regan pictured with Megan Mayhew, mother Lee, father Ronnie, and dogs Champ, Mr. Magoo, Princess, Lamar, and Bella

Reed Sorenson
Alvin, Brutus, and Zoe

"**F**or some reason, my family enjoys wiener dogs. They still have them. I had three different ones growing up; Scooter and Odie when I was younger, and my parents still have Lexi.

"I will never forget Odie. My dad bought him for my mom from the front of a grocery store. I thought he was the best dog. You couldn't pick him up or he'd make this loud yelping noise.

"Lexi used to go to the races with us. She has always liked to play ball and is still obsessed with a racquetball. She carries it around everywhere. She runs and plays so much. You can throw the racquetball and she'll act like a retriever. My parents also have Wrecks, that I've had since I was 12. He is a 115 pound Weimaraner.

"Now, I have Alvin, Zoe and Brutus.

"Alvin is a Shar-Pei. He does a lot of weird things. He is always trying to bury his bone in the bed on top of the sheets. Alvin is the only one of my dogs that sleeps in the bed, which isn't a good thing because he snores non-stop every night. And he's louder than most humans.

"Zoe sleeps on top of the table downstairs, I think to get closer to the fan. Zoe's a pit bull, and she will attack Brutus every once in a while. Brutus will jump in the lake and when he comes out of the lake, Zoe will just attack him. I don't know why she does it, there's really no reason, but she does.

"Not only does Brutus like the lake, but he is a Chocolate Lab who loves to play. He is obsessed with playing ball. We were at Lowe's Motor Speedway last year, and we were throwing the tennis ball for him. Brutus had run so much but wouldn't stop playing. I don't know if he got a cramp or something, but his back legs just gave completely out.

"I was worried, but that didn't stop Brutus. He had the ball in his mouth, kind of dragged himself over to me and dropped the ball, ready for me to throw it again. He didn't care that his back legs were just dragging the ground – he wanted to play. I have never seen anything like it in my life.

"Since I've grown up with dogs all my life, I think one of the worst things to see is when a dog has been killed on the side of the highway. I have seen a lot of that recently, and it's sad. To me, that's just an obvious sign that somebody didn't need to have that pet. That's why I think spaying and neutering is important.

"Anytime you can prevent an animal from being born that nobody's going to take care of, or prevent an animal from dying some sort of tragic death, I think that is a no-brainer. I don't know how much it costs to spay or neuter a dog now, I think you can get it really cheap or even free sometimes.

"I just don't want to see bad things happen to animals."

Shannon Spake
Dudley and Mylo

"**D**udley was my first dog. My husband Jerry McSorley and I started dating when Dudley was six-months-old, and he already had Dudley. We call Dudley, who's five, our privileged dog because we got him from the breeder.

"A couple of years later, we got Mylo, who's now three, from the pound by the airport in Charlotte. We were debating whether we wanted another puppy because we had already done everything with Dudley. We found a little girl puppy that we thought was so cute, but decided to go home and sleep on it. If we still wanted a puppy in the morning, we decided we would go back and get her.

"So we woke up the next morning, and went back to the pound. When we got there, Jerry said, 'Give me a second, I'm just going to run through to see what else is back there.' He came back and said 'Shannon, there is a dog back there that looks just like Dudley did when he was a puppy.'

"They brought him in and we met him. He was about eight weeks old. They said they found him and his whole litter underneath someone's grill behind their house. It was very sad.

"Mylo was so nervous, he couldn't even lift his hind legs off the ground, and he had a tennis ball in his mouth. We were sold. Thankfully, somebody else was there looking at the little girl so she got adopted that day, as well.

"We got Dudley from a breeder, but, I personally would never get another dog from a breeder because there are so many dogs out there that need homes. When you go to these places and see them, it is so sad. And they are good dogs.

"It's so interesting to me – every dog that I have ever met from the pound or The Humane Society, it is almost like they know. They know that they sort of cheated something and they know how lucky they are to be where they are. There is just something about them – they are smarter. It's like they just get it. They realize.

"In my opinion, getting Mylo was the best thing we ever did because the dogs get along so well. Dudley has such a great disposition. He's so kind and friendly that when Mylo was a puppy, Mylo could literally take bones out of Dudley's mouth and Dudley would do nothing about it.

"They just really love each other. It's funny. Dudley's main focus is to find his next meal. He really has a mind of his own, and that dog will do whatever he wants. And Mylo just loves to play, and play, and play, but he listens and really responds to orders.

"That's one of the reasons I could teach Mylo to get the newspaper. I was running one day, and I saw this dog running toward the end of the driveway. It stopped, grabbed the newspaper and turned around and ran back. I thought it was the coolest trick.

"I immediately went home and just started teaching Mylo. I figured Mylo is really, really, smart and listens. So why not? I brought Mylo outside, and I put the paper in his mouth at the end of the driveway, and said 'good boy.' Then I told him to 'stay.' I threw the paper and told him to 'fetch' and he brought it back. I just kept moving up the driveway and then went into the house.

"It took me maybe half-an-hour to teach him how to do that. So now, every morning, we open the front door and tell him to 'fetch.' He runs out there, grabs the paper and brings it back. I sometimes say that one of the only reasons I get the daily newspaper is so that Mylo can fetch it.

"Dudley and Mylo are everything to us. They bring so much happiness into my life. When I'm lying in bed at night and Mylo jumps up there and cuddles with me, because he is a cuddler, or if it is just playing with them in the yard, they just bring us so much happiness and a lot of love." 🐾

"Dudley and Mylo are everything to us. They just bring us so much happiness and a lot of love."

Tony Stewart
Kayle, Deuce, Wyatt, and Wylie

"I've always loved animals. I didn't grow up with any pets, but I can remember when I was little, dogs that supposedly were mean or would bite, I would walk right up to and they would just wag their tails and I would not have a problem with them. I just always loved pets.

"Now that I'm older, I've been lucky enough to have birds, iguanas, rabbits, parrots, a tiger, a monkey, dogs, and cats. So I've pretty much had enough to build my own ark.

"I got my Chihuahua, Kayle, from a pet store in 2002. About three years ago, I got Deuce. We were doing a Home Depot appearance in Daytona Beach, Florida. When we got done with the appearance, we were leaving and one of the store associates had her puppy back there.

"Everybody was oooing and aahing over the dog. I got a hold of him, and he started getting antsy. I took him over to the grass and put him down so he could go to the bathroom. He followed me around and, no matter who called him, wherever I went, he went. When he was in my arms, he finally just laid down and went to sleep while I was holding him.

"The lady offered to give him to us for a Valentine's Day present. I told her that I couldn't take her dog, but if she still wanted to give the dog away in a week to call and we would come get him. We tried not to get our hopes up when we left the store, but we were really excited when we got the phone call that she really wanted to give him to us. So we flew from California all the way down to Daytona to get the dog and take him back home. We've had him ever since. It was kind of a cool deal because when he was a puppy, he had a white heart almost on top of his head, and the first time we saw him was on Valentine's Day. It was one of those deals where you felt like it was meant to be.

"Then two years ago, Eddie and Dana Jarvis gave me two cats, Wyatt and Wylie for my birthday. Eddie and Dana have two brothers who have the same parents but from a previous litter, and I really liked their cats. I'm allergic to cats, but these don't bother me. They don't have a high dander count.

"Now, with my property in Indiana, we have worked with our local Department of Natural

Tony pictured with dogs Deuce and Kayle

Right: Tony pictured with dog Kayle

Resources, so, through them, we are now raising abandoned fawns. Every year we adopt a new set of orphaned fawns and raise them. Then in the fall, we turn them loose into the wild.

"It's very gratifying to know that we're helping these deer build their immune systems and become healthy enough so that they can go out and take care of themselves in the wild.

"We really enjoy our time each summer raising these deer, but it's a double-edged sword. We're very proud, but at the same time it is very sad every time fall comes around and we have to turn them loose. That first day that we open the gate to let them out in the wild is probably one of the toughest days of the year for us.

"But it's very gratifying knowing that these deer possibly would not have made it without us raising them. There's a sense of pride and satisfaction there.

"So whether it's our dogs, our cats, our deer, or our fish we take care of in the lake – our animals come first. Our animals eat before we eat, and they have it better than we do.

"That's a situation that I don't think most people realize. When you have pets, these pets rely on you 100 percent, not only for food and water, but for love and attention, too. If you're going to have a pet, you have to know that they are becoming a part of your life because to them, you are their life." 🐾

Tony pictured with cats
Wyatt and Wylie

If you're going to have a pet, you have to know that they are becoming a part of your life because to them, you are their life.

Deuce gives a hug to a rescued fawn

Martin Truex, Jr.
Lexus

"**L**exus has a heck of a personality – I'll tell you that. Sherry and I joke all the time that we wish she could talk because we wonder what she is thinking. She is always up to something.

"Lexus is about eight years old. Sherry got her when she was in college before I ever met her. When Sherry and I started dating, Lexus became part of my family, too. She's pretty special to both of us.

"Like most yellow Labs, Lexus loves the water. She loves to swim. She can't decide whether she would rather swim in the lake or swim in the pool, so she does both. She is constantly coming in the house wet.

"If you let her outside, sometimes she will fake like she is going to go to the bathroom. She'll go out the front door and run around to the back and jump in the pool then come back to the door and come in the house all wet.

"I take her fishing a lot when I go, too, but it's difficult. She loves fish and when I catch a fish she goes absolutely crazy. She wants to eat it. She sits there and barks at me and jumps up and tries to grab them out of my hand. She goes absolutely bonkers for the fish.

"It's kind of funny. She loves riding in things. So when I take her in the boat, she sits in the middle seat right next to me. I can go as fast as I want, she doesn't care. She likes the wind flapping her ears. She even sticks her neck way out trying to get in the wind even more.

"It's the same deal with my Cub Cadet and the jet ski. If I start up a jet ski, and she's down at the dock and I don't put her on the jet ski with me and take her for a ride, she will bark at me until she can't see me anymore. She sits in front of me on the jet ski and leans with the turns and everything. It's pretty funny.

"Lexus travels to the track most of the time with us. When we fly in the airplane, she sits in her own seat and looks out the window like a human. It's unbelievable.

"She's got such a great personality and is so different from any other dog I've ever known. She's high maintenance sometimes. She's spoiled, but she's just funny. And she's really good at letting us know what she wants.

"She tries to trick us into feeding her more than we are supposed to. Like if Sherry feeds her and I come home, she tries to trick me into feeding her, too. She paws at her bowl, sits there and stares at me, and she gives me those sad little eyes.

"She just makes me laugh. Here she is trying to get seconds and thirds of food, and there are

others who are struggling to put food on the table for their family and pets. That's why the Martin Truex Jr. Foundation and the Ryan Newman Foundation have worked in conjunction with Second Harvest Food Bank of Metrolina to collect food for families and their pets.

"With the difficult economic times, we wanted to do something so families could put food on the table for themselves and so they could afford to keep their pets, too.

"Pets are part of my family. I've had big dogs since I was just a little boy. And pets are part of a lot of people's families. I can't imagine what it would be like without Lexus, which is why we wanted to help families and their pets through our foundation work if we could." 🐾

Martin pictured with Sherry Pollex and dog Lexus

❝*Sherry and I joke all the time about that we wish she could talk because we wonder what she is thinking. She is always up to something.*❞

Wendy Venturini
Al and Pirata

"**A** few years ago, I had a Miniature Pinscher named Harley. When I got the job in NASCAR, I was putting him in a kennel every weekend. Now, my dear friends Pat and Gwen Beattie have him. I was putting him in the kennel every week and I was just bummed. I literally was crying every weekend because I would drop him off on Thursday and pick him up on Monday morning.

"Gwen knew that it was really bothering me putting him in the kennel. I'm not saying that putting a dog in a kennel is bad, but it was really upsetting for me every weekend. One day she said 'We would provide a really good family for him.' They adopted Harley, and they have given him a great life and a great home.

"Gwen knows Jarrad's and my schedule, so she knows when we have time off and are at home. She will see if we want to watch him during the winter or off-weekends. We actually had him for a week over Christmas last year. Harley's a great dog, and has a great personality. He really has brought a lot of joy to my life.

"It was one of the most difficult things to do because, selfishly, I wanted to keep him, but I knew he would have a better life with Gwen.

"Both Jarrad and I travel the Cup circuit together. We're on the road every weekend which is why we don't have a dog, even though I really, really, really, really want one. It's just difficult with our schedules.

"So we have 'nephew dogs' – Al and Pirata. My brother Billy wanted a lazy, low-lying dog for the race shop, and that's how he got Al, who's a Basset hound. When Pirata was smaller, he had one patch over his eye that was more predominant, so they named him Pirata, the Spanish word for pirate.

"I joke around that the only pets I have are our deer outside. We live out in the country. We have probably six or seven deer, and a buck out there. We have deer corn, a salt lick, and a deer camera so we take photographs of them while we're gone over the race weekends. We will come back home and see what the deer were doing while we were gone.

"It's funny. They come right up to that camera. So I call those my pets – all the deer in the backyard.

"I have my birds, too. I have hummingbirds, blue birds, and yellow finches. Our blue birds nested by themselves in a tree. When we saw the nest, I told Jarrad I was so excited because I've never seen blue birds in our neighborhood. So now I want to do research and learn everything about them. I don't want them to leave.

Wendy pictured with husband Jarrad and dogs Pirata and Al

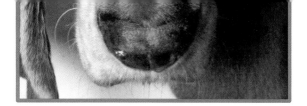

"Those are our pets right now. If you don't have a pet and can't have one if your situation or career, whether financially or socially, doesn't warrant it, then I think it is okay not to have a pet. That's being a responsible citizen, so to speak.

"The timing is not right for us now with our travel and how we travel. I think we're getting closer and closer to that family life and dog life, but it's just not right yet. However, if the situation arises, we will rescue a dog.

"I don't understand why people go out to these places and spend so much money on a pet, on a dog especially, when all these shelters have so many animals that need good homes.

"My best friend from high school has a rescued shelter dog. She's a Black Lab named Kayla and is the most gentle, well-behaved dog that I have ever seen. She's eight years old. I think a lot of times when people think of rescuing dogs – actually going to a shelter and rescuing an animal – they always think that there's got to be a reason why those animals are there, that they must be bad. And that's not the case. They're usually the sweetest and most-loving ones there.

"It would bring so much joy to me to take an animal out of a shelter that didn't have a home and a true family to watch over it every day. To be able to take that animal out of there, give it a home, and provide a family for it, that would be a pretty cool feeling. " 🐾

Above: Pirata

Right: Al

Brian Vickers
Caesar

"The best advice I can give to someone who wants to get a pet is, that I know you want to get a pet for you, but you've got to keep the pet in mind, and what is best for him or her.

"When I moved away from home as a teenager, I wanted a dog because I had grown up with small dogs. We had two Shih Tzu Tzus – Buffy was the mom and Trixie was the daughter.

"Growing up, Trixie would sleep at the end of the bed, and Buffy would lay right next to me all curled up. They were always fun. They both had a lot of energy and we played a lot growing up.

"I loved dogs, but getting one would have been irresponsible. I wouldn't have been able to take care of the dog or spend the time with the dog that it needed. Dogs need a lot of attention and have to be taken out, and it really wouldn't have been fair for me to get a dog. So, I chose a cat.

"Around the year 2000, I found Caesar, a full-blooded Siamese cat. Caesar is a very mischievous cat. I suppose all cats are to a certain extent, but he is extremely mischievous. He always wants to play and jump in your lap. He'll be sitting in your lap and you won't be paying attention, and he'll reach up and pop you with his claw just to get a reaction from you.

"Caesar is so friendly and loving, that to me, he is actually almost like a dog. He gets along with every person and animal he comes across. So, I guess I've got the best of both worlds.

"At the time I got Caesar, I had an apartment and I traveled a lot. It was perfect because a cat takes care of itself, so Caesar would stay at a home when I would be gone on the weekends. If I had to leave the house for a few days or just for the day, the cat can eat and use the bathroom and he's fine. You don't have to let him out. He doesn't need as much attention as a dog.

"Since I've had Caesar, I've actually found that I love cats as much, or more so than dogs. My decision wasn't based on what I wanted, but on what was best for the animal. I think you need that mutual respect. You are getting an animal, to a certain extent, for your own reasons because you want a pet, but you have to keep the pet's best interests in mind, too.

"And that's really the same reason why Caesar lives with my parents now – it's not what's best for me, but what is best for him.

"I moved to Florida and I'm traveling back and forth even more now, so Caesar mainly stays with my parents in North Carolina. I really think it is better for him. He seems much happier there. They have Trixie (the dog) that he likes to play and wrestle with; and my parents spoil him, too.

"Selfishly, I would like for Caesar to be with me all the time, but my lifestyle right now is not the best for the cat. I still get to see Caesar quite often, and I think he is happier with my parents. Caesar's happiness is what is important to me. 🐾

Krista Voda
Shelter Dog Ruby

"I have a unique perspective through my job when it comes to driver charities, NASCAR fans, and pets.

"I first became involved with Ryan and Krissie and the work their Foundation has done when I used to host the TV show "Totally NASCAR" back in 2002 or 2003. We did a feature on the Catawba Humane Society which Krissie and Ryan were helping at the time. We took a tour, and Krissie showed me all the things the foundation had contributed toward.

"Then in 2005, I went back to the Catawba Humane Society with the TV show "NASCAR Nation." Those were my first spotlight pieces on local projects in which the drivers were involved.

"All the guys travel so much in this business that everyone looks at NASCAR as such a nationwide event, you forget all the good they do locally, right in their own backyard and the differences they make at home. That was what really jumped out at me while visiting the Humane Society and seeing what an immediate impact the foundation was making.

"One of my favorite events to help with is "Partner for Paws" at Daytona with Ryan and Krissie's Foundation (Ryan Newman Foundation) and the Greg Biffle Foundation. I knew there were a lot of pet lovers who were NASCAR fans, but I was amazed at the number of people at that event. All the people would come up and tell me about their dog or their horse or their birds

– every animal that they have. It is just a great event and the drivers are able to raise a lot of money for their charities.

"For me, the connection between NASCAR and pets is natural. Everyone always talks about how NASCAR is such a family sport. And, for anyone out there who has a pet, I know from growing up with dogs and cats, that our pets were a part of our family.

"It's only natural that your pets go on the road. Obviously, NASCAR is a little different. When the fans come out in their motor homes, tents, or campers, they basically live at the racetrack for an extended period of time.

"It's a couple of days where they pick up and bring the comforts of home with them. You wouldn't think to come out to a race and not bring your pet if it is do-able, if it can travel or if you have the means to do so. So, it is a lot different than the NFL where the fans show up a couple of hours before the game and then go home afterward. This is where people are camping out and living at the racetrack. And, if you're going to make it your home away from home, you have to have your pet with you.

"Growing up, our pets were part of our family. We had a dog in the house at all times. We had a Collie named Cocoa, like Hot Cocoa,

66For me, the connection between NASCAR and pets is natural. Everyone always talks about how NASCAR is such a family sport. And, for anyone out there who has a pet, I know from growing up with dogs and cats, that our pets were a part of our family.99

who stayed outside and we had a mutt named Tippy who stayed inside. When they passed away, we got Oreo, who was a little black dog that was a house dog.

"At one point, we had Oreo the dog, Chi-Chi the cat, Winston the Cat, and Chad the Cat. Our house had animals coming in and out all the time.

"I don't have a pet now because my fiancé and I travel. We would love to have a dog. Every time I see a little one, I want to take it home, but we haven't mastered the concept of leaving and who would take care of the dogs just yet.

"We are an Aunt and Uncle to our friends' yellow Lab named Milo. We help watch him during the week because we have weekdays free.

"When our friends went to the hospital to have their baby, the first thing I did was run over to the house and take Milo for a walk because I knew he wouldn't be the center of attention anymore. So I went over to give him some last minute attention before his new little baby brother came into the house.

"Although we don't have any pets in the house right now, we live on almost two acres of land with a lot of wooded area, so we have a lot of wildlife in our backyard. I have a couple deer and turkey that come through the yard on almost a daily basis. Those are kind of our pets.

"We have salt licks and apple blocks in our yard so the deer will come and have a safe place to hang out.

"Some days it's almost like a postcard with birds, butterflies, and turkeys crossing the yard. The deer come out, and we have chipmunks running across the yard, too. It's really cool. Because we travel so much and can't have the indoor pets, at least we have the wildlife out there. We like to think those are our pets." 🐾

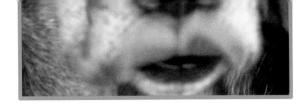

Darrell Waltrip
Olivia, Trusty, and Badger

"**S**tevie and I have had animals our entire married life.

"This is an old story but Charlie Brown was probably the most favorite dog I have ever had. Charlie Brown was a long-legged Dachshund.

"Stevie had given me a Dachshund for Christmas right before we got married and her name was Duchess. I lived in an apartment, and I didn't have time to take care of Duchess, so my mom and dad took care of Duchess.

"Well, Duchess was out on the sidewalk one day, and I reckon we'll never know what kind of dog happened to go by, but whatever the dog was – he was a traveling man, we know that – and he got Duchess pregnant and she had six puppies.

"We gave all of them away except Charlie Brown – he was the only brown one in the litter. He was a little male, and so we decided we'd keep him. We kept Charlie Brown, and he was like our child.

"He went everywhere with us. He rode in the tow truck. That was when we were just getting started. I had my own team, and Jake Elder was my crew chief.

"Charlie Brown would go with us to all the races. He traveled everywhere we went. If we stayed in a hotel, we'd put him in a box and slip him in there. He slept with us down at the bottom of the bed. He was just the coolest little dog in the world.

"Now we have Olivia and Trusty, who are our 11-year-old Basset Hounds and Daisy, who's just a mutt.

"We bought Olivia and Trusty from the pet store. We were not looking for dogs, and we walked by the pet store, and you know how they put the dogs in the window? Well, one of the Basset Hounds was in the window.

"So we got the dog and took her into that little room where you visit with the dogs, and Olivia was so cute. She was in there running around and playing, being a little puppy. About that time, the person that runs the store brought another one back there to us. So now we have two, a male and a female.

"They played together. They rolled on the floor. They chased balls. Trusty was crazy. He would grab the ball, run around and knock Olivia over. He was just wild. He was a wild man, but cute as he could be with those long ears. So we went there, not looking for any dogs, and we left there with two.

Darrell pictured with wife Stevie, daughters Jessica and Sarah, and dogs Olivia and Trusty

❝I always recommend to people looking for animals to go to the humane shelters because they're good places. You can get some great dogs that make great pets at the humane society.❞

"The girls found Daisy here in the neighborhood. Somebody had abandoned her as a little puppy. They picked her up and brought her home, and we kept her. She's a stray that turned out to be the better of the three actually.

"We even have rats now. When Stevie told me that Jessica (who is in college at Belmont) was bringing home two rats, I asked, "is there no other pet that she could attach herself to other than a rat?" She rescued these lab rats that were going to be put down at school.

"I never knew anybody that had a pet rat. I wasn't really excited, but they're alright. They're just weird looking. They've got a little nose and beady red eyes. I wouldn't necessarily want to have one as a pet. But that's my girls.

"And I guess I wouldn't have it any other way. Pets have been very important to our family. We help the local humane society and Happy Tails here in Franklin, Tenn. That's where I got Hobie Cat for Stevie for an anniversary present.

"I always recommend to people looking for animals to go to the humane shelters because they're good places. You can get some great dogs that make great pets at the humane society.

"And when you get them, make sure you spay and neuter them. All our pets have been spayed or neutered. I think it is important to control what your animals do. It's good for them." 🐾

Sarah and Jessica pictured with horse Badger

Michael Waltrip
Copper and Jack

"Ever since I've been on this Earth, we have had a dog in our house. We have always been dog people. The first dog I remember was a little Dachshund named Duchess. She must have been a baby when I was born because we had her until I was 14 or 15.

"After Duchess, we got another Dachshund named Samantha. I called her Sam. Sam was deaf. For a long time, we just thought Sam wasn't smart or that she wouldn't listen to us. But eventually, we found out that she couldn't hear. If you didn't know Sam was deaf, you would have thought my parents had lost their minds.

"They would be out there stomping their feet and saying 'Sam' and waving at her, trying to get her to come. I just remember watching them act like that and trying to take care of poor Sam.

"Since I grew up around animals, I think they are just a normal part of the family. Macy has Copper, a Quarter Horse, and Jack, a Dachshund-Poodle mix.

"Macy got Copper when she was nine years old, and she has been riding him ever since. At the barn, if Macy gives Copper a treat, he'll stick his nose in her pocket to try to get more treats.

"Macy made the finals at a barrel race on Copper. Since she did so well, she got a puppy. She named him Jack because she got him in Jackson, Mississippi.

"Jack just loves Macy and all people. When someone walks in the door, he gets so excited that he runs around in circles and just wags his tail constantly.

"We have always taken care of our pets. They have always been spayed or neutered. In my opinion, it's important to control the population. There are so many dogs out there that need a home and we don't need to add to the problem, so we try to do what we can.

"It's just so important to help, because there are not enough homes for all the dogs, and that's sad. You've got to take care of your dogs, and hopefully have the compassion or the heart to take care of others as well, if given the chance.

"Adopting a pet or going to the pound to get a dog is something that's important to me. I think that's a pretty neat way to go about getting your next pet." 🐾

Macy with horse Copper

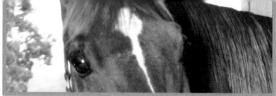

Michael and daughter Macy, and dog Jack

Michael pictured with daughter Macy, horse Copper, and dog Jack

66 *It's just so important to help, because there are not enough homes for all the dogs, and that's sad. You've got to take care of your dogs, and hopefully have the compassion or the heart to take care of others as well, if given the chance.* 99

Shannon Wiseman
Prince

"**I** adopted Prince two years ago when he was two and he is the light of my life.

"Prince is a Bichon Frisé. He was the product of a divorce, which happens to a lot of dogs. My friends split up and neither one of them wanted Prince, so I decided to take him.

"I'll admit that he is spoiled rotten. His favorite thing to do is 'go bye-bye.' I have a car seat for him with a seat belt so it keeps him really secure but it also allows just his head to go out the window because he loves the wind in his hair. Prince is my partner in crime.

"We go everywhere together. He loves to walk. He also loves to meet people. He's the most social dog I've ever seen. It's like he is running for president wherever we go. Prince just wants to be loved, and he has this power over everyone and everybody loves him.

"Because I travel so much, I share custody of Prince with my Mom. If you're in NASCAR and you're staying at hotels, it's just really not feasible or practical to take a dog on the road. So when I'm away my Mom, who is divorced, has an empty nest of sorts and keeps Prince for me. Prince is kind of someone for her to care for.

"She's always liked dogs, but they were just dogs until Prince came along. Now it is different. She really has this huge affection for Prince, more so than she ever thought she would have for a dog. Now, she is the most proud grandmother in the world. She calls Prince her little baby boy. 'Prince, my boy, my baby boy' – is a little song that she sings for him.

"I'm the youngest in our family, so I always used to get presents and little knick-knacks here and there from Mom, but now my dog gets them. I will come over to the house and she will say 'Look what I bought for Prince.'

"She bought him a special bed that is blue and shaped like a crown with his name on it in white. He won't sleep in that bed because he likes to sleep on our face pretty much, right on our shoulder at night. But he keeps all his toys on the bed – it's like his toy box.

"It's the same thing with my Dad. My Dad is a manly-man. He is 6'3". He is from the mountains of North Carolina. He grew up on a farm with hunting dogs.

"He never had a dog on his lap or one that was all cuddly or affectionate, that just wasn't my Dad. But the first time he watched Prince, he fell in love with him. The second time I took Prince over to see him, my Dad had carved his name 'Prince' into a wooden sign, painted it white,

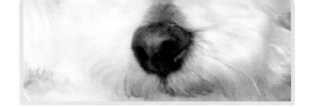

and added sparkles. You know that Prince has affected your Dad if he is painting something and adding sparkles. That's just the power that Prince has over people.

"Knowing that, no matter what, I have someone that loves me unconditionally is the best feeling in the world. I grew up with all kinds of different pets. And through the years, have volunteered at different Humane Societies in Gaston County (NC) and in Atlanta. I used to go walk dogs because they needed people to do that, and for me, I wanted to be around dogs and feel that love.

"I truly believe that dogs are man's best friend. They embody love."

"People are going to disappoint you in life. And you're going to disappoint yourself. That's just human nature. Having a dog or a cat is knowing there is one little thing in your world, that, when you come home, no matter what has happened, he loves you unconditionally. That's the best feeling in the world."

Matt Yocum
Gipper, Dutch, and Sam

"**I** don't remember a time when I didn't have a dog in my life.

"Although I've had Labs and even a St. Bernard, I think my family's love for Cocker Spaniels dates back to my grandfather, Earl Keller. Years ago, he brought a black Cocker puppy to my mom, who was four or five at the time. He came into the house empty handed, with the puppy in his jacket pocket. I can visualize the expression on both their faces when my mom realized there was a puppy struggling to get out of the pocket. She and my grandfather named him Tippy because of his white-tipped tail.

"I had a couple of black Cocker Spaniels when I was a very small kid. Rusty was a blonde/red Cocker that I had in my early teens and then Clancy was a blonde Cocker that joined our family during my senior year in high school. The Gipper arrived in 2000.

"In the past couple of years, The Gipper has welcomed two additional members to the family. You see Gipper loves to travel to the races to visit with his friends. Winston, who belongs to Terri Parsons and her late husband, Benny, was one of Gipper's best buddies. Seeing Gipper so happy playing with Winston, made me realize that he would love a buddy to play with when he was home. I found two black Cocker Spaniel brothers, Dutch and Sam. They rode home with me completely silent. All you could see were four little eyes peering through the dog kennel.

"The three of them have become 'The Yocum Gang.' All three dogs are similar in so many ways, yet each has his own distinct personality.

"The Gipper, well he's still The Gipper. He still likes to travel to races, still loves people, and his buddies. His day is complete if he can ride in the truck with the window down, head outside and his ears just flying in the wind.

"Dutch is the most sensitive and loving of the three, but because of his heavy coat, he prefers to lounge in the AC. However, regardless of the heat, if I'm in the yard, Dutch is right there with me.

"Sammy is the smallest of the three, yet he is the guard dog of the gang. He loves to lie on the back deck waiting for a golfer to come into view. If anyone hits a ball near the fence, he immediately goes into action; racing down to the fence to inform them they're not to come into his territory. When he's satisfied that he's made his position clear, he returns to the deck very proud of his security patrol to await the next foursome.

"They're all determined to be the first out the door the instant they know I'm headed for the

truck. Seniority does have its privileges though – it is understood among them that The Gipper always gets the front seat and the Banditos ride in the back.

"The greatest thing about the dogs is they're always your best friend. They love unconditionally. They're also dependent on us for their most essential needs.

"Following Hurricane Katrina, the Newmans loaded every inch of a motor home with food, and Krissie drove off to New Orleans to help with the many abandoned pets. Because of the Newmans, their Foundation, and their commitment to animals, people are becoming more aware of getting their pet spayed or neutered, and hopefully, one day the overpopulation issue will no longer exist."

The greatest thing about the dogs is they're always your best friend. They love unconditionally. They're also dependent on us for their most essential needs.

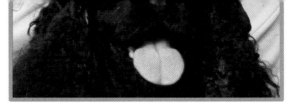

The Fan Pages

No sport would exist without its fans. NASCAR fans are some of the best fans in the sporting world. Fortunately, they are just as passionate about their animals as their drivers! Our *Pit Road Pets* team travelled to Bristol Motor Speedway, Charlotte Motor Speedway, and Michigan International Speedway to meet these dedicated fans. We were overwhelmed with the turnout and the stories each fan shared with us about their furry family members. We appreciate how each fan shared their stories and allowed us to include them in our *Pit Road Pets* book. Thank you and we hope you enjoy the Fan Pages.

Top row, left to right:
Bob and Carolyn Howald
with Angel; Jackie Greene
with Mimi; Sandra Cochran
with TJ, Baby, and Jeter.

Bottom row, left to right:
Jackie Morgan with Harlie;
Connie and Marvin Houchins
with Champ and Freckles; John
Forester with Magie.

Top row, left to right:
Vickie and Steve Knable
with Mingo; Scott and Misty
Lalonde with Cooper and
Jäger; Anne Manfull with
Duchess and Miracle.

Bottom row, left to right:
David and Jacqueline Mullin
with Hoss; Roger Peck with
Splat, Teddy, Sweetie, Hemi,
Angel, Harley, and Wooki;
Leslie Randall and Jeff Hall
with Sam, Reece, and Simba.

Top row, left to right: Debbie Sayer and Brandon Casey with Romy and Buster; Carol Clause with Tori; Jamie Scheirer with Georgia.

Bottom row, left to right: Matt-Sale, Ann and Dexton Howell-Davis with Buster and She-Ra; Michelle Hunt with Dakota; Danette and Myles Cook with Hank.

Top row, left to right: Sandra and Denk Hicks with Maddi; Cherry and Gary Matthews with Scogbie; Justin and Zachary McDaniel with Delilah.

Bottom row, left to right: Jamie Robertson with Kimber (hearing assist dog); Walter and Georgia Britton with Jacob; Wesley Mutter with Lexi.

Top row, left to right:
Steve Wilson with Casie;
Frank Marko with Shelby;
Danielle Davison with
Hunter.

Bottom row, left to right:
Colleen Curtis with Dobby;
Logan and Vickie Vega with
Jasper (African Hedgehog);
Brianna Vega with Crush.

Top row, left to right: Sheryl and Terri King with Lily; Bill Frank with Bailey; Champ Boucher.
Bottom: Amanda Jones with Champ.

Top row, left to right: Laura Nichole Belliveau with Lenny; Kim and Caitlin Gray with Lucy; Sean Carvey and Mary Keith Brooks with Maggie.

Bottom row, left to right: Dave Stockham and Kris Ehlinger with Elwood; Kim and Kyle Brown with Chloe; Jody and William Jones with Winston, Rudy, and Missy.

Bristol

Top row, left to right: Sally and Robert Kepfer with Spirit and Adobe; Gloria Chamberlin with Smoke; Rebecca Meier, Cassandra, and Shane Pickering with Max.

Bottom row, left to right: Harold Cinqmars with JD; Micah and Michael Scobee with Maggie; Danette and Mark Cook with Hank.

Bristol

Top row, left to right: Lisa and Pete Culotta with Dora; Deb Fox with Wylie; Dominic Giovanetti with Daisy; Mischelle L. Goodman with Buddy.

Bottom row, left to right: Jason Hahn and friend with Tekyo; Debbie and Geoff Harwood with Riley and Maverick; Susan C. Hollis with Chalupa; Thomas Hoover with Ozzie.

Bristol

Top row, left to right: Shari Jones, Skip Spencer, and Bella; Jeanne Kamansky and Timber; Joseph and Joe Kemesky with Stosh (a pig); Marlene and Gary Kirkendall with Abby and Honey.

Bottom row, left to right: Earnest Laughlin with Freckles; Susan Laughlin with Bailey; Cynthia Marcus with Sadey; Dr. Deci McIver with Shiner.

Bristol

Top row, left to right: Rita and Joe Mumford with Lucy and Daisy; Terri Mizer with Bomizer; Ronald Oleson with Dallas; Heather and Craig Peterson with Nukag and Nevada.

Bottom row, left to right: Tony and Tamara Rickli with Ozzy; Jennifer, Bryan, Ethan and Noah Snyder with Rowdy; Kelly Stull and Susan Moore with Jada; Kasey Kuhl with Sammy Belle.

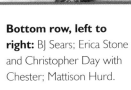

Top row, left to right: Debra Swanson with Austin and Robin; Lisa and Joseph Treadway with Scooter; Randy Vess with Baby Girl; Robert and Ryan Williams with Brook and Bristol.

Bottom row, left to right: BJ Sears; Erica Stone and Christopher Day with Chester; Mattison Hurd.

Top row, left to right: Rodney Shelton with Oscar Mayer; Cindy and Dan Lyon with Tosha; Margie Woodall with Holly, Buddy, and Annie; Alberta and Brian Ouellette with Bubba, Maggie, Molly, and Tucker.

Bottom row, left to right: Calvin Bahr with Shawnie; Emily and Jay Baumhardt with Bitty and Belle.

 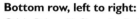

Michigan

Top row, left to right: Anastasia and Scott Denton with Tessa; Nick Hill with Juno; Terry and Shelly Eland with Arvey, Fancy and Elby.

Left: Herbie Hall with JD and Cheyenne.

Bottom row, left to right: Brian and Kim Hart with Jay; Janet McDowell with BB; Tracy and Jim Osterhout and Family, with Lucy.

Michigan

Top row, left to right:
Allison Quade with Stella;
Deborah and Tim Laczek
with Abbi; Butch Rhores with
Dale (Pygmy Diary Goat).

Middle row, left to right:
Janet and Dean Martin with
Samson; Timothy and Kelly
Waller with Jazmine.

Bottom row, left to right:
Susan Pedrick with Kirbie;
Karen Hatcher with Fuzzy;
Michelle, Meaghan and
Brittani Shew with Newman.

Top row, left to right: Kari Snemis with Kiko; Jennifer and Amanda Stamford, Ryan Kowalski with Dozer; Sue and Elise Strait with Moe; Marylou Ericks with Snoopy.

Bottom Row, left to right: Linda Castillo with Cloie; Susan Sutak with Winston; Unidentified Michigan fan; Mike Howard with Buster.

Acknowledgements

The making of *Pit Road Pets, the Second Lap* was a group effort of numerous animal lovers who believed in our foundation's mission. We greatly appreciate everyone who has helped us make this edition of *Pit Road Pets* possible.

To the drivers, crew chiefs, NASCAR personalities and their families who made the time in their busy schedules for our photo shoots and interviews, we would like to give our most sincere appreciation. This book would not have been possible without you. Thank you for making *Pit Road Pets; The Second Lap* a reality.

We would like to thank all of the people who helped us schedule and organize the photo shoots for *Pit Road Pets; The Second Lap*. Including, Van Colley, Russell Branham, Lee Smith, Janice Goss, Kelley Earnhardt Elledge, Billy Race, Montgomery Lee Petty Schlappi, Cindy Caldwell, Rory Conellan, Chris Williams, Shannon Adams, Maggie Martin, Mary Barr, Sarah Holladay, Sherry Clifton, Kristine Curley, Emily DiNunzio, Benny Ertel, Lori Halbeisen, Beth Hart, David Hart, Lisa Hartsell, Lynn Hess, Traci Hultzapple, Amanda Jones, Eddie Jarvis, Jodi Toomes, Kendra Jacobs, Matt Masencup, Jennifer Shelley, Stephanie Atwood, Jodi Geschickter, Jennifer Chapple, Toni Schermerhorn, Judy Shriver, Bill Janitz, DeLana Harvick, Sherry Pollex, Lynne Allmendinger, Buddy Baker, Ashley Allgaier, Wayne Auton, Robin and Lisa Pemberton, Dick Berrgren, Eva Busch, Vickie Compton, Beth Gibson, Lindy Hornaday, Jay Howard, Lisa Johnson, Katie Kenseth, Claire B. Lang, Tati Papis, Doug and Robin Richert, Lisa Reutiman, Angie Skinner, Shannon Spake, Wendy Venturini Egert, Krista Voda, Jamie Christianson, Matt Yocum, and Shannon Wiseman.

A special thank you to those special people who worked behind the scenes and gave us the support needed to make this book a success – Kevin Donaldson, Mike Horvath, Annette Vanderhoff, Kathy Halik, Cheryl Hanna, Mary Grams, Michelle Croom, Pat and Mary Svanson, Greta Anderson, Lisa Merrick, Ann-Marie Dameron, Katie Dodd, Whitney Duncan, Kris Partlett, Heather Shew, Philip Lyon, Mike Arms, Catherine McNeil and John Farrell, Carolyn Miller, James and Joanne Boyle and Theresa Doles.

We offer our gratitude to the animal rescue groups and humane societies that provided us with beautiful and loving animals for our photo shoots: Noah's Ark (Locust Grove, GA) Diane Smith, Paula Hedgecoth, Jama Hedgecoth, Shenan Griffin, and Laura White; Kitty City/Cabarras Cares (Concord, NC) Patsy Beeker; Cascades Humane Society (Jackson, MI) Debra Carmody; Humane Society of Catawba County (Hickory, NC) Jane Earnest; Anheuser Busch- Budweiser (St. Louis, MO); Helen Woodward Animal Center (Rancho Santa Fe, CA) Mike Arms, Margo Caskey, and Renee Simmons.

A special thank you to Mike Arms, you are an inspiration to me and I value your guidance. Thank you for sharing your story and being a special part of *Pit Road Pets; The Second Lap*.

Thank you to Michigan International Speedway, Charlotte Motor Speedway and Bristol Motor Speedway with allowing us to open up the opportunity for NASCAR's fans to be a part of this book.

And a huge Thank You to the Fans of NASCAR, who not only support *Pit Road Pets* by purchasing the book, but also took the time to come to our track photo shoots and allow us to take their photos with their beloved pets. NASCAR fans are truly the best! 🐾

Yours Truly,
Krissie Newman

Photo by Larry Hill, Nashville, TN

About the Photographer
Karen Will Rogers

A California native now living in Nashville, Tennessee, Karen Will Rogers has an illustrious career photographing some of the biggest names in the music and entertainment industry. She has a natural ability to capture the emotional essence of her clients.

However, this unusual gift is not just reserved for humans. One of her most passionate and acclaimed talents is her unique way of catching the delightful personality traits of animals. Her skill in making these irreplaceable moments has made her one of the most sought-after pet photographers in the industry.

With a deep desire to share this special art form with the world, Karen has already finished two photography books on celebrities with their pets. The first book, Music Row Dogs and Nashville Cats, published by Simon and Schuster, gives an inside look into the lives of many beloved country artists with their companions.

Pit Road Pets, published by the Ryan Newman Foundation, gives the NASCAR fan a rare look at some of the biggest names in the world of racing with their animals.

Karen has teamed up with the Ryan Newman Foundation once more for Pit Road Pets: The Second Lap, a delightful collection of photos and fun-loving, sometimes poignant tales of animal devotion by some of the most admired names in NASCAR along with their families.

"Witnessing and capturing the love between these families and their pets has been an intriguing and deeply stirring experience for me," Karen said. "There is nothing quite like the bond between an animal and its owner. It moves my heart to be a part of such a special project giving a voice to all animals that so profoundly deserve to be loved, wanted, and celebrated."

Karen lives with her 3 pups: Wilson, Maggie, and Nickey. Visit her on the web at www.karenwillrogers.net.

Karen Will Rogers would like to personally thank…

My mother who was always there with her love and support. The rest of my family: my Dad, Robert, John, Billy, Lori, Brittany, Tammie, Johnny, Christopher Williams, Ashley, Bryon, Madelyn, Bird, Uncle Dan, Aunt Grady, Aunt Donna, Uncle Ted Vargo, Aunt Sharon, John Zoppa, Carol Espey, Mickey Bryant, and Rose Hein.

Larry Hill for caring for my pups when I travel and for taking my photo! Brandon and Ashley Giles, Wendy Woods, Tracy Peskorz, Robert and Beth Weedman, and Angela Justice your support, thank you! Stacy Williams thanks for writing my bio for the book. Carol and Billy Roach, your friendship is treasured. Mike Wolfe (soul friend), Frank Fritz, and David and Nickie Nuding, I will always be thankful for the opportunity to do my first book deal at Simon and Schuster.

Laura Lacy for your friendship. Carolyn Miller, Bridgette Tatum, Philip Lyon (attorney), Hanna Family, Mary Grams, Michael Horvath, Greta Anderson, and Mary Svanson; Lisa Merrick and Ann Marie Dameron for all your help at race shoots.

Theresa and Joe Diffie for their love of animals. Nancy Lee Andrews, Brenda Melendez, and Holly Nance; Dina Dembicki for a great book layout. Russ Wright for your artwork. Vincent A. Brown for your retouching and Brannon Bishop. Michelle Croom, my adventures with you on the photo shoots were memories of a lifetime! Rob Croom, thank you always! Kortney and Preston Kappel, Matthew Grove, Peter and Diane Nesbitt, Debbie Cross from Kenny Rogers' office and the entire Rogers family. Todd and Jack Butcher, Veda Radanovich, Joe Deborda, and Dury's photo lab, Nashville.

There are not enough words to express all that Krissie and Ryan Newman do for animals. Your passion and grace are such an inspiration to me. I am so grateful and excited about being on the Pit Road Pets Team. Thank you so much!

About the Writer
Wendy Belk

Everything Wendy Belk tackles in her life, she does with passion. She is a dedicated professional involved in the sport of NASCAR racing and has worked in a variety of positions as a public relations representative in the Camping World Truck Series, Nationwide Series, and Sprint Cup Series over the past decade.

Belk, a West Jefferson, N.C. native and graduate of the University of North Carolina-Chapel Hill, began working with Ryan Newman during the 2008 NASCAR Sprint Cup Series season. She describes her most memorable professional moment as working with Newman when he won his first Daytona 500 on February 17, 2008 at Daytona International Speedway.

But, as passionate as Belk is about her job, the absolute loves of her life, in addition to husband Michael, are her dogs Levi, a Black Labrador and Nicky, a Yellow Labrador mix. So when the Newmans, Ryan and wife Krissie, needed someone to write Pit Road Pets, Belk knew it was something she had to do. Being involved with "Pit Road Pets: The Second Lap" combined a number of passions – the sport she loves, writing, and pets.

"There's nothing like coming home from a weekend on the road, and being greeted with kisses from Levi and Nicky – no matter what time it is," Belk said. "My dogs are just like my kids. They mean the world to me, and they seem to make everything better."

Belk currently works for True Speed Communication, handling the public relations efforts on behalf of the No. 39 Stewart-Haas Racing team and resides in Mooresville, N.C.

Wendy Belk would like to personally thank...

My husband, Michael, who I am so lucky to have. I could never thank him enough for being my better half, for putting up with me and for taking care of our dogs all the times that I'm not home. I love the crazy little life we have!

My Mom and Dad, Mark and Dwenda Goodman, who give me more love and support than I could ever repay them for. I wouldn't be where I am today without their constant encouragement and love.

My little sister, Misti Rose, who is the best gift that I ever got that I didn't ask for. She brings more joy and laughter to my life than anyone could imagine.

Jenny, thank you for being you and for allowing me to be me. You keep grounded, and you let me soar. I'm so grateful that I have a friend like you that I count on no matter the time or place. I thank my lucky stars for our friendship every day.

Mike Arning and all of my co-workers at True Speed Communication thank you. I have the best job ever, and a lot of that is because of the people that I have the pleasure of working and spending so much time with.

And finally, to Ryan and Krissie, I can't thank you enough for everything. Ryan, you keep me on my toes, and that's a good thing! Krissie, I'm in awe of the passion that you have for not just the animals and the Foundation, but for all the projects that you tackle. You are amazing. I have thoroughly enjoyed working with both of you these past few years and I look forward to many more. I truly was honored that you entrusted me to help with this project. Thank you for that. I count myself very fortunate to work with people who I consider part of my extended family. 🐾